Penguin Critical Studies
Advisory Editor: Bryan Loughrey

F. Scott Fitzgerald

The Great Gatsby

Kathleen Parkinson

Penguin Books

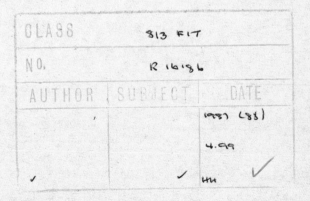

PENGUIN BOOKS

Published by the Penguin Group
Penguin Books Ltd, 27 Wrights Lane, London W8 5TZ, England
Penguin Books USA Inc., 375 Hudson Street, New York, New York 10014, USA
Penguin Books Australia Ltd, Ringwood, Victoria, Australia
Penguin Books Canada Ltd, 10 Alcorn Avenue, Toronto, Ontario, Canada M4V 3B2
Penguin Books (NZ) Ltd, 182–190 Wairau Road, Auckland 10, New Zealand

Penguin Books Ltd, Registered Offices: Harmondsworth, Middlesex, England

First published in Penguin Masterstudies 1987
Reprinted in Penguin Critical Studies 1988
10 9 8 7 6 5

Printed in England by Clays Ltd, St Ives plc
Filmset in Monophoto Times

Contents

Note

Page references in this study are to a 1984 Penguin reprint of the text. Earlier texts have a page extent of 192, while 1984 and later texts have an extent of 172. The Twentieth-Century Classics edition uses the same page numbering as 1984 and subsequent editions but also includes a critical introduction.

1. *The Great Gatsby:* A Novel of the 1920s

After achieving success and recognition with the publication of his first novel, *This Side of Paradise*, in 1920, Scott Fitzgerald chose both to identify his writing career with the ebullience and optimism of the decade, and also to be its keen critic. The hedonistic mood of the 1920s came to an end with the Wall Street crash of 1929, which was followed by a period of economic suffering and misery for millions of Americans in the biggest consumer society in the world. Fitzgerald identified his own declining creativity with this deterioration. In the early 1920s, however, for a young man not too long demobbed from the army, who was to be dependent on his writing for a living and knew what it meant to be hard-up, literary acclaim brought the satisfaction of knowing that he could write. A further happy result was that Zelda Sayre, whom he had met while he was an officer in the army, agreed to marry him now that his future seemed assured. Even so, for a young couple given to extravagant living the sales did not bring in enough money, and he quickly found that he could command high prices for his short stories. A recent biographer expresses the dilemma which, as a serious novelist, Fitzgerald faced through the 1920s.

As a writer Fitzgerald had to live by the pendulum because as soon as he stopped grinding out pulp for the big magazines and turned to serious writing he found himself on the brink of financial disaster. His independence was measured by the number of stories he had to produce each year. But his dependence increased with his needs, which grew grander by the year; the temptation to take the easy way was reinforced by the rapidly rising fees he commanded, especially from the [Saturday Evening] Post.[1]

It is significant that a good story like 'A Diamond as Big as the Ritz' (see the Penguin collection of stories published under that name) was refused by this magazine because it was critical of American materialism. Only optimistic stories were wanted for popular consumption. As a writer sensitive to the times Fitzgerald wanted to be a serious critic of the society in which he lived, and yet he longed for commercial success too. Already in 1922, when he was twenty-five years old, there is evidence in his diary of inner tension.

A bad year. No work. Slow deteriorating depression with outbreak around the corner.[2]

Critical Studies: The Great Gatsby

The Jazz Age: 'It was borrowed time anyhow'

Fitzgerald was regarded, however, by readers of the *Post* as *the* writer who best represented images of the new post-war generation of ambitious middle-class Americans wanting to enjoy the consumer spending boom of the 1920s. His stories seemed to express the dream world which advertising was busily constructing: jazz and dancing; young flappers who cut their hair, smoked and drank – new women; romantic night-life. Above all, his characters were consumers who spent lavishly and extravagantly. As its most successful contributor of stories, Fitzgerald helped to create the rapid success of the magazine.

In their early married life the Fitzgeralds seemed to embody the new Jazz Age, and Fitzgerald wrote both himself and his wife into some of his short stories as well as into his next novel, *The Beautiful and Damned* (1922). But both drank heavily and they were often in debt, despite the income from the film rights of several stories. Moreover, there seems to have been a mutually destructive drive in their relationship, as each egged the other on to extremes of rashness and irresponsibility; yet each needed the other. The Fitzgeralds' own lifestyle provided a wealth of material for the novel he was working on. In 1922 they returned to New York from the Midwest, where they had gone for the birth of their only child and where he could work in peace. They rented a house in Great Neck, Long Island, across the bay from where the old-established millionaire families of the first industrial boom in the late nineteenth century had their summer homes. There is a measure of correspondence here to Fitzgerald's fictional locations of West Egg where Nick Carraway lives, and East Egg where the Buchanans' estate is, but Fitzgerald superimposed his own geography on a real locale.[3] A number of great estates existed along the shores of the island, many being taken over in the 1920s by theatre and film personalities, newspapermen, songwriters and musicians, along with a few rich bootleggers. One such figure was the financier Edward Fuller, who achieved notoriety at the time Fitzgerald was planning Gatsby's financial activities. The Fitzgeralds themselves entertained on a large scale, their parties sometimes going on for several days. Le Vot constructs what he regards as a typical scenario for the social life they led at this time, though he does not provide any sources, and one must read it as a biographer's dramatic fiction with some basis perhaps in personal memoirs.

Fitzgerald, with a bottle of champagne clamped under his arm, escorting screenwriter Anita Loos [*Gentlemen Prefer Blondes*] into the Plaza in search of Zelda and a friend, only to be chucked out for being too drunk; sharing the warm champagne with the three women in the taxi taking them to Great Neck, interrupting dinner to show out a woman admirer who had forced her way into the house; being so annoyed at a remark by Zelda that he pulls out the tablecloth, sending dishes and glasses crashing to the floor, whereupon the ladies retire to the living room; falling asleep under a tree and waking to join them at tea, whereupon the evening proceeds in the coziest affability.[4]

Doc Civet or Miss Baedeker, guests at Gatsby's second party (pp. 102–3), would have felt at home.

Lavish consumption and hedonistic display were acceptable activities in the 1920s. Advertising on a new national scale encouraged Americans to buy, and to get rich quickly was not merely an aspiration but a possibility, even a requirement. Corruption was widespread. Members of the administration were implicated in scandals involving fraud and bribery; other scandals had for some years involved city politicians and police in corruption relating to the control over prostitution and gambling empires. One figure who reigned in the underworld until his murder in 1928 was Arnold Rothstein, whose life bears some resemblance to the fictional figure of Meyer Wolfshiem in *The Great Gatsby*. One of Rothstein's friends, Herman Rosenthal, had betrayed his police connections in New York to the press in 1912, and was subsequently murdered at the door of the Metropole Hotel. A police lieutenant called Becker was executed with others for this crime, as Wolfshiem reminisces on p. 69[5] of *The Great Gatsby*. Rothstein seems to have managed his protection racket more successfully than Rosenthal, and it is thought that if he did not actually pull off the great coup of the White Sox Fix of the World Series (Baseball) in 1919, he knew of it and bet accordingly.[6] But profits from such exploits were as nothing beside the rewards from bootlegging – the manufacture and sale of illegal liquor – after the Prohibition Bill of 1920.[7] This Bill represented a final attempt by the old-established puritan faction to legislate public morality on the issue of drinking, but it was never backed by adequate provision for law enforcement by the federal government. In fact, it achieved exactly the opposite of what was intended: not only did people manage to acquire as much liquor as they wanted, they actually lost respect for the law and traditional moralities, as the lines of demarcation between legal and illegal, moral and immoral, became confused. In the novel, Gatsby and Wolfshiem bought up backstreet drug-stores to create a network of outlets in New York and Chicago (p. 127), and Gatsby has a very useful understanding with the police commissioner (p. 67).

It is clear that Fitzgerald found ample material to hand in the years 1922–4 in preparation for his novel. One of his neighbours in Great Neck was a stockbroker named Edward Fuller, who had suddenly sprung into prominence in 1921 under the patronage of a leading stockbroker, C. A. Stoneham, owner of a racetrack, a casino, and a newspaper as well as a majority share in the New York Giants baseball team. Fuller had influence with the police and was one of the first residents of Great Neck to own and fly his own plane. He was charged with gambling away his customers' funds and selling non-existent shares by telephone. All kinds of further scandals surrounded the several trials concerning his activities, including suborning or kidnapping of witnesses. Officials in respectable institutions were implicated in a vast network of graft and crime. Fitzgerald was interested in the case and followed all the newspaper reports.

In 1931, in an article called 'Echoes of the Jazz Age',[8] Fitzgerald identified other peculiarly American characteristics of the 1920s:

We were the most powerful nation. Who could tell us any longer what was fashionable and what was fun? . . .

Scarcely had the staider citizens of the republic caught their breaths when the wildest of the generations, the generation which had been adolescent during the confusion of the War, brusquely shouldered my contemporaries out of the way and danced into the limelight. This was the generation whose girls dramatized themselves as flappers, the generation that corrupted its elders and eventually overreached itself less through lack of morals than through lack of taste. May one offer in exhibit the year 1922! That was the peak of the younger generation, for though the Jazz Age continued, it became less and less an affair of youth . . .

A whole race going hedonistic, deciding on pleasure . . .

The word jazz in its progress towards respectability has meant first sex, then dancing then music. It is associated with a state of nervous stimulation, not unlike that of big cities behind the lines of war . . . In any case, the Jazz Age now raced along under its own power, served by great filling stations full of money . . . It was borrowed time anyhow – the whole upper tenth of a nation living with the insouciance of grand dukes and the casualness of chorus girls . . .

The metaphorical use of 'filling stations full of money' and 'borrowed time' in this passage picks up key ideas in *The Great Gatsby*. By the early 1920s the motor car was a newly established feature of American life that represented affluence and seemed to offer a new freedom. It has an important presence in the novel as both status symbol and destructive agent. Time, both as history and as a psychological state, is central. No doubt Fitzgerald had the very specific setting of the novel in the summer of 1922 in mind when writing the articles, and his judgement that this was the peak year of the Jazz Age is related to his novel, but in any case he was always an acute social observer. Jazz itself is a case in point: 'Vladmir Tostoff's Jazz History of the World' (p. 51), which is played at Gatsby's party, asserts that jazz is an authoritative and authentic voice of the period which not only has a place in history but is *the* modern art form to express it. It was an essentially American one.

The bandleader Paul Whiteman was one of the earliest exponents of jazz to reach an international audience. He wanted to give it respectability by creating a new art form, symphonic jazz. Having achieved success on Broadway in 1920, he was encouraged in 1924 to put on a jazz concert in a symphony hall which he called 'An Experiment in Modern Music', the major composition being Gershwin's 'Rhapsody in Blue'. It was later repeated at Carnegie Hall, by which time Whiteman was billed as 'The King of Jazz'. Among other songs that Whiteman recorded in the early 1920s are 'Three O'Clock in the Morning', Daisy's song at the end of Gatsby's second party (pp. 104–5), and 'The Love Nest', one of the two songs Klipspringer plays while Gatsby and Daisy sit in ecstatic reunion (p. 92).[9]

Elsewhere in his writing Fitzgerald spotted a tension between the generations exemplifying old traditional values and those expressing the new hedonism in America, which he locates in *The Great Gatsby* in the provincial Middle West and sophisticated urban New York respectively.

The uncertainties of 1919 were over – there seemed little doubt about what was going to happen – America was going on the greatest, gaudiest spree in history and there was going to be plenty to tell about it. The whole golden boom was in the air, – its splendid generosities, its outrageous corruptions in the tortuous death struggle of the old America in Prohibition. All the stories that came into my head had a touch of disaster in them – the lovely creatures in my novels went to ruin, the diamond mountains of my short stories blew up, my millionaires were as beautiful and as damned as Thomas Hardy's peasants.[10]

Fitzgerald saw the city, not the rural scene, as essentially the setting for any representation of modern American traumas and personal tragedies in the post-war years.

New York

As in all his novels, Fitzgerald combines in *The Great Gatsby* a keen eye for social details with an intensely personal imaginative response to place. In an article called 'My Lost City', first published after his death but clearly written during the Depression years of the 1930s, he recalls his own sense of wonderment when visiting New York as a boy and young man. He, too, like Nick Carraway, was a provincial, so dazzled by the city that he 'took the style and glitter of New York even above its own valuation'. When he came to live in New York in 1919 after army service, it 'had all the iridescence of the beginning of the world' for an impoverished and unknown young man. After his success in 1920, as the spokesman of the emerging 'young generation', he noted and gave a place in his fiction to such new social phenomena as the cocktail party, the speak-easy, the flapper (though she was *passée* by 1923). He and his wife would drink a quart of Bushmill's whisky and then go 'out into the freshly bewitched city', through strange

doors into strange apartments with intermittent swings along in taxis through the soft nights . . .

They might find themselves summoned out to Griffith's film studio on Long Island, where

we trembled in the presence of the familiar face of the *Birth of a Nation*; later I realized that behind much of the entertainment that the city poured forth into the nation there were only a lot of rather lost and lonely people.[11]

Such memories resemble Tom and Daisy's reaction to the star and her director at Gatsby's second party (p. 101), or Nick's response to summer evenings in the city (p. 57).

Long Island lies to the east of Manhattan, and two of its boroughs, Queens and Brooklyn, are incorporated into the city. The island covers over 17,000 square miles and today has a population of over 7 million people. The western end of the island is a densely suburban area with an industrial concentration in Long Island City. The north shore, looking out over the Long Island Sound, has been called the 'Gold Coast' because it attracted so many wealthy landowners who built great estates there along the coast. The south coast contains a number of fashionable resorts, such as Southampton, where Jordan Baker goes visiting (p. 147).

The population of Long Island doubled between 1920 and 1930, as bridges and tunnels to Manhattan made industrial development and commuting possible. Wilson's garage and Michaelis's café mark the beginning of this, forming the growth of a Main Street (p. 27), but as yet they have no name (p. 133). From 1910 onwards the Queensboro Bridge (p. 67) and the East River tunnel of the Pennsylvania Railroad (p. 40) gave direct access to Manhattan. During the 1920s the area known as Flushing Meadow (the name is a memento of those Dutch sailors who first came there (p. 171)), which had originally been marshland along the Flushing River, became a city refuse dump and open sewer. By the 1920s trainloads of trash and garbage arrived daily from Brooklyn, and may well have given Fitzgerald his idea for the valley of ashes (p. 26).[12]

Some of the earliest American films were made out on Long Island at the Astoria Studios before Hollywood became the centre for the new industry, these studios employing such international stars as Gloria Swanson, the Marx Brothers and Rudolph Valentino.

In *The Great Gatsby* Fitzgerald gives New York prominence as the centre of American fashion, wealth, entertainment, crime (along with Chicago) and social exclusiveness, using a wealth of detail which locates the city precisely in the early 1920s. Yet his style always surprises and delights the reader with the suggestion of a secret dimension of the city which is magical and mysterious, particularly in the opening part of the novel when the time is early summer and there is a mood of hope and optimism. For example, Nick finds Fifth Avenue 'warm and soft, almost pastoral' (p. 30). A short while afterwards Gatsby's great limousine, 'with fenders spread like wings . . . scattered light through half Astoria' (p. 66) before crossing the Queensboro Bridge to give a view of 'the city rising up across the river in white heaps and sugar lumps all built with a wish out of non-olfactory money'. The final phrase presumably means that the wealth which built the skyscrapers was none too savoury in its origins, yet it is immediately followed by a set of contrary implications.

The city seen from the Queensboro Bridge is always the city seen for the first time, in its first wild promise of all the mystery and the beauty in the world. (p. 67)

The 'white heaps and sugar lumps' are the skyscrapers which give New York its unique skyline. No other city in the world can compete with its vista of shoreline and skyline, and Fitzgerald was justified in presenting it as a source of excitement to Nick. In the 1920s New York was beginning to contribute authentic American features to the images of the modern world which are now a common heritage.[13]

However, it would be a mistake to read *The Great Gatsby* as primarily a social record. For one thing, the authentic background material is filtered in selectively and given a symbolic or psychological significance. Contemporary corruption and hedonism are not the central theme of the novel, and in a letter written in 1937 Fitzgerald defined their function thus:

. . . in *Gatsby* I selected the stuff to fit a given mood or 'hauntedness' or whatever you might call it, rejecting in advance in Gatsby, for instance, all the ordinary material for Long Island, big crooks, adultery theme and always starting from the *small* focal points that impressed me – my own meeting with Arnold Rothstein for instance.[14]

It is worth bearing in mind that rather strange term 'hauntedness' when trying to define the qualities of the novel. This will be considered in later chapters, in particular Chapter 2.

Although *The Great Gatsby* mirrors features of the life of wealthy pleasure-seeking New Yorkers in the Jazz Age, it is also representative of two other aspects of the contemporary artistic scene. First, it is set in the aftermath of the First World War and, like other works of the period, gives expression to a mood of disillusion with the institutions of society and despair at its loss of values. Second, it is a consciously experimental work by one of the young post-war generation of American writers who visited Europe and were aware of new literary ideas and achievements associated with Modernism. They wished to contribute a specifically American theme to literature by giving new artistic intensity and significance to the language they used.

The post-war mood

When Daisy asserts her membership of the 'rather distinguished secret society' of the disillusioned, Nick with some justice dismisses this as facile:

'You see I think everything's terrible anyhow,' she went on in a convinced way. (p. 22)

The novel offers far more convincing images of desolation and despair than Daisy could know of. The valley of ashes, first introduced on p. 26, which obtrudes its presence upon travellers by road and rail, acts as a powerful symbol of a callous, careless society and of its underlying despair. It is a huge dumping ground for the detritus of a modern industrial society totally absorbed in materialism, which the many references to dust and ashes link inextricably with sterility and death. Nick sees the ash-heaps as an obscene parody of natural, life-enhancing growth which creates a bizarre landscape where grey ghostmen move about and where George Wilson lives as a sick failure reduced to the status of a ghost. The area functions dramatically too as the location in which all the characters' lives meet and collide, with catastrophic results. The brooding eyes of Doctor T. J. Eckleburg are blind to human misery.

The 'wasteland' is a recurrent symbol of social and personal sterility and despair in the writing of the 1920s. T. S. Eliot's poem *The Waste Land* (1922) offers the most well-known example of a sustained set of images of universal and individual sterility and emotional failure. Eliot draws on Old Testament imagery of desert, stones, and dryness, but builds on these a whole range of images which create a collage of dramas about the pain of isolation, of being unable to love or to differentiate between experiences. Many of these vignettes of pain and isolation are set in scenes of the contemporary post-war world, though Eliot's concern is not only with this.

Ernest Hemingway, Fitzgerald's slightly younger contemporary, also published a variation on the theme at about this time, a deceptively and puzzlingly simple story called 'Big Two-Hearted River' (1925). The only character is a young man called Nick Adams, who in other stories sees service in the trenches of Europe and is now taking a solitary fishing-trip. What is characteristic of the story is the restraint of Hemingway's non-committal style, which forces the reader to ponder the significance of a seemingly slight sequence of actions. Nick Adams seems to find emotional peace in the solitude of the open countryside when he is forced to exercise total self-control in setting up his tent, cooking his food and absorbing himself in the habits of the trout he is trying to catch, creatures existing outside himself. Yet before he reaches the river, which in the story seems to offer emotional peace, even salvation, he has to make his way over an expanse of black, burnt terrain. No explanation is offered, and the reader has to determine how far this waste area symbolizes some trauma which is both public and personal to Nick.

After the war, which had brought thousands of Americans to Europe for the first time, many stayed on or soon returned there to lead expatriate lives, Fitzgerald and Hemingway among them, because they could not accept the old ways of provincial life at home. Gertrude Stein, herself an expatriate, is said to have remarked of the post-war generation:

A lost generation of men and women adrift in a chaotic hell of their own solipsism.[15]

Hemingway created just such characters in the novel, *The Sun Also Rises* (1927): his expatriate men and women engage in a frenetic pursuit of excitement and thrills to stop themselves having to face the terror of their own emotional bankruptcy. Some of them have moved beyond the limits of respectable society. Brett, the major woman character, with her emancipated, rather mannish styles of dress and speech, sleeps around, yet she is tortured by her fear of her own lack of feeling. The other central figure, Jake, an American journalist, is the only character who achieves any equilibrium in his life, but, significantly, he does so because he is impotent as a result of a war wound which has symbolic implications.

In *The Great Gatsby* Tom and Daisy have tried the expatriate life.

They had spent a year in France for no particular reason and then drifted here and there unrestfully wherever people played polo and were rich together. (p. 11)

They are members of the 'lost generation', but their great wealth insulates them from awareness of this. They are indeed 'adrift in a chaotic hell of their own solipsism', but they enjoy their privileges too much to be potentially tragic in the manner of Hemingway's characters. They are merely unattractive.

The post-war voice

In 1924 the Fitzgeralds set sail for Europe in a bid to escape the way of life which had brought them into debt and prevented serious writing. Just before setting off, Fitzgerald wrote to his editor, Maxwell Perkins:

> I feel I have an enormous power in me now, more than I've ever had, in a way, ... so in my new novel I'm thrown directly on purely creative work – not trashy imaginings as in my stories, but the sustained imaginings of a sincere yet radiant world. So I tread slowly and carefully and at times in considerable distress. This book will be a consciously artistic achievement and must depend on that as the first books did not.[16]

Fitzgerald was always responsive to the voices of serious literary and cultural criticism in the 1920s. Two very influential figures at the time were H. L. Mencken and Edmund Wilson, both of whom urged the need for a national literature which could express the complexities of modern life, though their approaches were very different, as were their influences upon Fitzgerald. In 1921 Fitzgerald said he would rather have Mencken like one of his books than anyone else in America. In an essay called 'The National Letters', Mencken had deplored the typical hero of American popular novels as a figure whose role was essentially to achieve 'what, under a third-rate civilization, passes for success'[17] rather than to resist social pressure and thereby fail. Mencken therefore looked for social criticism and strong social awareness in literature and a real sense of moral crisis. He was for some years editor of a magazine called *The Smart Set*, which with a blend of wit and irony set out to criticize the prevailing American materialist values, and gave space to controversial writers in order to stimulate intellectual debate. However, his comment to Fitzgerald on *The Great Gatsby* – 'The story is fundamentally trivial'[18] – is surely misguided.

Edmund Wilson, a contemporary and friend of Fitzgerald, was just beginning to establish his formidable reputation as an American man of letters in the early 1920s. In June 1921 he wrote to Fitzgerald of the obstacles to the growth of American artistic life in a materially rich but artistically new nation:

> I do think seriously that there is a great hope for New York as a cultural centre; it seems to me that there is a lot doing intellectually in America just now – America seems to be actually beginning to express herself in something like an idiom of her own. But, believe me, she has a long way to go. The commercialism

and industrialism, with no older and more civilized civilization behind except one layer of eighteenth-century civilization on the East Coast, impose a terrific handicap upon any other sort of endeavour: the intellectual and aesthetic manifestations have to crowd their way up and out from between the crevices left by the factories, the office buildings, the apartment houses, and the banks; the country was simply not built for them.[19]

Wilson had his finger on the pulse of American cultural life and he was right.[20] For the first time in its existence America was beginning to assert its identity in an international context. Jazz, a musical medium with its roots in the lives of poor black Americans and owing no debt to European traditions, was creating a new style. The skyscraper, as I have suggested, was an essentially American phenomenon. The American film industry, more than any other, was beginning to create a mass culture which exercised an international influence in shaping ordinary people's images of themselves.[21] In responding to modern European art American artists created a style of their own. Wilson gave intellectual weight to the recognition that America constituted a cultural phenomenon of the twentieth century and as such needed to enter the mainstream of twentieth-century literature. New York was the new pivot of such activity, and *The Great Gatsby* gives significance to the city as a magnet in the post-war years.

It was Wilson who introduced Fitzgerald to such experimental European works as T. S. Eliot's *The Waste Land* and James Joyce's *Ulysses*, both published in 1922, while he was working on *The Great Gatsby*. Fitzgerald was also reading the novels of Joseph Conrad during this period, and was particularly struck by Conrad's technique of deploying a single narrator who, like Nick Carraway, is both participant and observer. He was interested too in Conrad's techniques of selection, by means of which every detail carries a range of significant, often symbolic meaning.[22] Conrad's language is rich in sensuous and symbolic reference; time is frequently fractured to represent the psychology and inner world of central characters. Fitzgerald consciously sought such effects in his novel.

A brief comparison with a contemporary novel whose theme is similar will show just how much Fitzgerald was working in, and indeed creating, a new American literary idiom. Theodore Dreiser's *An American Tragedy* was also published in 1925, but its techniques are essentially those of saturation rather than selection. The narrative documents the life from boyhood to death in the electric chair of Clyde Griffiths. Like Gatsby, Clyde comes from an impoverished and arid environment in the Middle West which is bare of all beauty or aesthetic interest. He is drawn towards a meretricious, exclusive, snobbish society in the East, whose only concern is its own material wealth and status. In order to maintain his precarious foothold in this glamorous world of careless power, he eventually plans to murder the factory girl who is pregnant by him and is demanding marriage. Whether he actually murders her is not clear, though she certainly drowns. When Clyde is charged with murder the moral outrage of the nation is unleashed against him as violator of traditional values of family and womanhood, though the real motivation is political. Clyde is used and exploited by a number of conflicting interested parties. Dreiser's narrative deploys the accumulation of details, scenes, characters and conversations to achieve a realistic effect. His primary concern is the relationship between character and environment, and he needs to create a web of institutional and social interaction by means of multiplicity of incident and realistic detail in order to show that the morally naive Clyde is betrayed by society.[23]

Fitzgerald shared some of Dreiser's interests. Mencken misjudged the novel when he termed it trivial, for it is a bitter, savage satire on the moral failure of the Jazz Age which is placed within a perspective of American images of success and American history. His techniques of selection and his narrative structure enable Fitzgerald to move easily between the elements of social realism and the symbolic landscapes to define the moral chaos of a society which has rejected any values but wealth. Despite the iridescent gaiety and colour pervading the earlier part of the novel, the overall effect offers a bleak affirmation of the difficulties of attaining a mature moral vision amid the hedonism and limitless, almost fabulous, wealth of modern America.

2. A Novel of Intricate Patterns

something new – something extraordinary and beautiful and simple and intricately patterned . . .[1]

Fitzgerald shaped the surface action of the novel by means of social gatherings – dinner, lunch and tea parties, wild parties, drunken parties, and the final aimless jaunt to New York in Chapter VII. Yet these achieve much more than the mere portrayal of a hedonistic society and, in particular, a group of people bent only on the gratification of their own desires. The gatherings are given significance through the central presence of Nick Carraway's discriminating judgement, through the sharp contrast between the landscapes and through the poetic power of the language. The profusion of social gatherings in itself constitutes a meaning: social life is both all-important and chaotic. Only Gatsby cherishes an inner life, but it is based on a dream.

The organization of *The Great Gatsby*

Time

Fitzgerald creates uncertainty for the reader about how to judge Gatsby by means of the narrative organization, and this uncertainty mirrors Nick's own feelings and dilemma. The charismatic and ambivalent figure of Gatsby is the centre of interest to Nick and to all the guests who gossip about him as they enjoy his lavish hospitality. His interest for Nick changes constantly as new aspects of his personality are revealed, the reader being present at the unravelling of the threads of information or illumination by which Nick is finally enabled to construct a coherent image of him. The story of Gatsby's past emerges piecemeal for Nick, allowing him finally to recognize parallels in his own impulses and desires.

The chain of events is slight until the three violent deaths of Myrtle and George Wilson and Gatsby bring them to a climax. The main focus is psychological, as Nick ponders on aspects of Gatsby's personality and in the process confronts his own ethical identity too. Fitzgerald frequently fractures time in the novel by drawing upon recollections by Gatsby, Daisy, Jordan, Michaelis, Wolfshiem or Mr Gatz. Time thus becomes a major feature of the narrative: in the events of that summer of 1922 the passage of time is recorded in some detail, yet events in the past keep exercising an interest which interrupts the present, just as the story of Gatsby's past keeps intervening because of that moment in time when his imagination invented a radiant self which he needs to reclaim.

'Can't repeat the past?' he cried incredulously. 'Why of course you can!' (p. 106)

The actual events of the novel cover a period from roughly 1907 to 1924. (Gatsby is 'a year or two over thirty' (p. 49) in 1922, and it would therefore have been about 1907 when, as a seventeen-year-old, he had his momentous meeting with Dan Cody. Nick is recalling the events of 1922 some one/two years later as narrator.) A chronological account would have required Fitzgerald to make a systematic representation of nearly twenty years of Gatsby's life. Instead, he concentrates very precisely on four months from early summer to autumn in 1922, inserting at various points details of Gatsby's past. Such fracturing of time heightens the intensity of emotion experienced by both Gatsby and Nick, creating in the novel a poignant sense of what is lost or unattainable, an ideal self which would be no longer at the mercy of powerful contradictory desires.

THE CHRONOLOGY OF EVENTS PRECEDING 1922 IN *The Great Gatsby*

These emerge through various personal reminiscences which are sometimes given directly in the text, sometimes reported by Nick.

12 September 1906	Young James Gatz of North Dakota (aged about 16?) writes his ambitions into a schedule and set of resolutions.	Ch. IX, p. 164
1907–12	Jay Gatsby is 'born' when James Gatz, aged seventeen, meets Dan Cody and is invited aboard his luxurious yacht *Tuolomee*: he stays there in a vague personal capacity for five years, until Cody dies and Gatsby is tricked out of his inheritance of $25,000 by Ella Kaye.	Ch. VI, pp. 94–5
October 1917	During the war Jordan Baker meets Daisy Fay in Louisville, Kentucky, with Lt. James Gatsby.	Ch. IV, pp. 72–3

1917–18	Gatsby and Daisy have an affair, and he experiences a transfiguring moment as he kisses her.	Ch. VI, pp. 106–7
	Gatsby rises to the rank of major and is decorated for bravery in battle.	Ch. IV, pp. 64–5 Ch. VIII, p. 143
February 1919	Daisy marries Tom Buchanan of Chicago. A letter from Gatsby, who is still in Europe, arrives just before her wedding, and momentarily makes her change her mind.	Ch. IV, p. 74
February 1919	Gatsby is at Oxford for five months, worried because Daisy won't wait for him.	Ch. IV, p. 65 Ch. VII, p. 123 Ch. VIII, p. 143
Summer(?) 1919	Gatsby revisits Louisville after Daisy's marriage and grieves over his loss.	Ch. VIII, p. 145
Summer(?) 1919	As a penniless young man just demobbed, Gatsby meets Wolfshiem in Winebrenner's poolroom on Forty-third Street, New York, and asks for a job.	Ch. IX, p. 162
August 1919	After the honeymoon, Tom has an affair with a hotel maid in Santa Barbara, California, and both are involved in a car crash.	Ch. IV, p. 75
April 1920	Daisy's daughter Pammy is born.	Ch. I, pp. 21 2 Ch. IV, p. 75

THE SUMMER OF 1922: EVENTS IN THE MAIN NARRATIVE
There are many precise details concerning time during the period June–November.

1. Early June: 'in two weeks it'll be the longest day of the

Critical Studies: The Great Gatsby

year' (p. 17) when Nick dines with Tom and Daisy
Buchanan.   **Ch. I**

A few days before 4 July (p. 29) Nick spends the even-
ing in Tom and Myrtle's flat in New York.   **Ch. II**

2. 5 July 1922 (p. 60): Nick writes out his list of the guests
   that summer at Gatsby's parties on an old time-table.   **Ch. IV**

3. 'One morning late in July' (p. 62) Nick lunches in New
   York with Gatsby and Wolfshiem.   **Ch. IV**

4. Two days later (the day after tomorrow (p. 80)) Daisy
   comes to tea with Nick and meets Gatsby again after
   nearly five years.   **Ch. V**

5. 'For several weeks' (p. 98) Nick does not see Gatsby
   until he calls one Sunday and Tom happens to drop in
   with Mr and Mrs Sloane.   **Ch. VI**

6. 'The following Saturday' (p. 100) Daisy and Tom come
   to Gatsby's party.   **Ch. VI**

7. 'One Saturday night' (p. 108) the lights fail to go on in
   Gatsby's house.   **Ch. VII**

8. 'Next day' (p. 108) Gatsby telephones with an invita-
   tion from Daisy for lunch 'tomorrow'.   **Ch. VII**

9. 'The next day' is broiling! (p. 109). This is the day of
   the New York trip and their drive back 'toward death
   through the cooling twilight' (p. 129).   **Ch. VII**

10. 'It was this night' (p. 141), after Myrtle Wilson's death,
    that Gatsby recalls to Nick his meeting with Dan Cody
    and his love affair with Daisy. It is Nick's thirtieth
    birthday (p. 129).   **Ch. VIII**

11. 'It was nine o'clock when we finished breakfast' (p. 146)
    the next day and Nick goes to his office in New York.   **Ch. VIII**

12. That same day Michaelis keeps Wilson company until
    six o'clock before going home to get some sleep
    (p. 152); 'four hours later' Wilson has gone (p. 152);
    for three hours he disappears from view; 'By half-past
    two he was in West Egg' (p. 153).   **Ch. VIII**

13. 'At two o'clock Gatsby put on his bathing suit' (p. 153).   **Ch. VIII**

14. The butler waits for a telephone message 'until four o'clock' (p. 153).   Ch. VIII

15. Nick decides to take 'the three-fifty train' (p. 148) from New York. He rushes anxiously up the front steps of Gatsby's house to find Gatsby dead in the pool.   Ch. VIII
Ch. VIII

16. 'On the third day' (p. 158) after this a telegram arrives from Mr Henry Gatz from a town in Minnesota. It is a 'warm September day'.   Ch. IX

17. 'One afternoon late in October' (p. 169) Nick meets Tom Buchanan on Fifth Avenue.   Ch. IX

18. 'I spent my Saturday nights in New York' (p. 170).   Ch. IX

19. 'On the last night' (p. 171) Nick visits Gatsby's house. By now it must be November, and the summer residences on Long Island are closed.   Ch. IX

1923–4: AFTER THE MAIN NARRATIVE

Nick is 'writing' the story: he speaks of returning from the East 'last autumn' (p. 8) and later says 'After two years I remember the last of that day' (p. 155). (There appears to be a slight discrepancy about the actual time when Nick is writing.)

Ch. I

Ch. IX

The narrative is organized in social occasions, some of which parallel others or create a contrast with them. For instance, Daisy's luncheon party in Chapter VII creates echoes of her dinner party for Nick in Chapter I; Myrtle's activities as hostess in Chapter II are a contrast to Daisy's sophistication in the previous chapter; Gatsby's two parties in Chapter III and Chapter VI are perceived differently by Nick because of Daisy's presence at the second. The weather, too, moving from the soft breezes of early summer through the intense heat of late summer to autumn, contributes to the different moods of the various occasions.

A SUMMARY OF EVENTS

Ch. I (pp. 7–25)   Nick introduces himself as narrator, referring to his return to the Middle West from the East 'last autumn', that is, the autumn of 1922. He comments on Gatsby, 'the man who gives his name to this book', as possessing 'some heightened sensitivity to the promises of life', and thus makes Gatsby the focus of interest. He also initiates one of the time shifts in the novel by recalling how he went East in the spring of 1922 to make a career (or fortune) in stockbroking, and came to be living in a shabby bungalow at West Egg on Long Island. The action begins here in early June 1922. Nick is invited to dinner at the elegant home at East Egg of his distant cousin Daisy Buchanan and her husband Tom, 'two old friends whom I scarcely knew at all', and there he meets their guest Jordan Baker. The visit reveals barely concealed tensions between Tom and Daisy, and gives Nick a glimpse of a luxurious but frivolous and trivializing way of life. On returning to West Egg, Nick sees his unknown neighbour Mr Gatsby standing alone, gazing intently across the water at a distant green light.

Ch. II (pp. 26–40) On the way to New York one Sunday afternoon a few days later, Nick is compelled by Tom Buchanan to visit a garage on the edge of a desolate area Nick calls the valley of ashes. Here he meets Tom's 'girl', Myrtle Wilson, the proprietor's wife, and is pressured into accompanying them to the flat Tom rents in a lower-middle-class area of New York. Myrtle is determined to act the grand hostess, and the party she gives parodies Daisy's entertaining. It ends violently when Tom savagely breaks Myrtle's nose because she insists on repeating his wife's name. They have all been drinking heavily.

Ch. III (pp. 41–59) At West Egg Nick is invited to Gatsby's party one warm summer night. He listens to a variety of whispered rumours about his host before actually making his acquaintance. Gatsby invites Jordan Baker inside the house for a private conversation, and when she returns she says she has just 'heard the most amazing thing'. In the following weeks Nick begins to like New York, and he embarks on a closer relationship with Jordan.

Until this point little has happened. All but one of the eight characters have been introduced into the narrative; Meyer Wolfshiem is yet to appear, and so nothing is known of Gatsby's business activities. Certain tensions underneath the entertaining and party-giving which constitutes the first three chapters have been established. Much of the narrative consists of banal or frivolous conversations among strangers or acquaintances, and quite often they are drunk: they gossip or pass on extravagant rumours about Gatsby, and most of them add their own. Nick's role is that of unobtrusive but ironic observer as they fantasize or try to deceive themselves or each other.

It is a mark of Fitzgerald's skill that he maintains the interest of all these vignettes of rather ludicrous, drunken strangers and at the same time makes the conversation contribute to the significant tone of the novel and to its major themes. There is an underlying sense of violence as well as self-deception or unreality in the lives of these characters which seems to be an adjunct of all the party-giving.

Ch. IV (pp. 60–78) During a drive to New York with Nick, Gatsby tells him 'God's truth' by filling in details of his childhood 'like a young rajah ... collecting jewels, chiefly rubies, hunting big game ...' and later as a young officer in wartime service in France and at Oxford. Nick remains sceptical until Gatsby produces a medal for gallantry and a photograph of himself at Oxford in aristocratic company. As narrator of his early past, Gatsby is clearly romanticizing, but there is truth in the rest. Over lunch he introduces Nick to a business acquaintance, Meyer Wolfshiem, who 'fixed the World's Series (a major baseball league) in 1919' and played with 'the faith of fifty million people'.

At this point Jordan Baker becomes narrator of a scene which took place in October 1917 when she met her friend Daisy Fay with a young officer named Jay Gatsby in their home town of Louisville, Kentucky. She tells Nick of Daisy's subsequent marriage to Tom Buchanan and of his early infidelity. She explains that Gatsby has bought his house 'so that Daisy would be just across the bay'. She is acting as intermediary for Gatsby, who wants to meet Daisy at Nick's cottage.

Ch. V (pp. 79–93)   This chapter is placed at the centre of the organization of the novel. Nick's tea-party for Daisy begins as comedy in the rain and ends with Gatsby's ecstatic reunion with her. Already, however, Nick wonders whether the real Daisy – whose frivolity has already been revealed to the reader – can live up to Gatsby's dream of her.

Ch. VI (pp. 94–107)   Interlude: At this point Nick narrates what Gatsby tells him 'very much later' about his self-transformation from the penniless young drifter James Gatz, aged seventeen, into Jay Gatsby. He had seized his destiny when he warned millionaire Dan Cody that his yacht was anchored in a dangerous spot on Lake Superior and charmed his way into a position on board. The actual conversation takes place on the night before Gatsby's death, and so in fact Nick knows nothing of Gatsby's past until then. As far as the actual participants are concerned Gatsby's past is unknown, but the reader is placed in a privileged position. Gatsby's second party is attended by the Buchanans, and Nick senses 'a pervading harshness that hadn't been there before'. Nick recounts what Gatsby tells him after the party, walking 'up and down on a desolate path of fruit rinds and discarded favours and crushed flowers', of his wartime affair in 1917 with wealthy Daisy Fay which culminated in his committing himself to her as if he were following 'a grail'.

It is significant that Gatsby is never the narrator of his own story, other than his fictitious childhood or a little about his wartime service. Nick always narrates what Gatsby has told him, thus synthesizing and giving coherence to emotions that Gatsby would probably never have been able to express. This has the effect of keeping Gatsby as the central focus of the narrative and giving significance to a love story which might otherwise seem over-sentimental. The language describing the second party conveys a change of mood in the narrative: words such as 'harshness', 'septic', 'desolate' and 'discarded' introduce a new note which is sustained until the end.

Ch. VII (pp. 108–39)   Daisy and Gatsby are lovers again, though this is intimated only indirectly by Gatsby's closing his house to guests: Fitzgerald omits any account of their affair.

On a broiling hot day, 'almost the last, certainly the warmest, of the summer', Daisy invites Gatsby and Nick to a luncheon party. The tension rises as Tom guesses the truth. In a desperate mood of escapism they drive aimlessly to New York and book a suite at the Plaza Hotel. Gatsby is determined to force a showdown and claim Daisy, but he is defeated by Tom's brutal social arrogance and Daisy's need of the assurance of Tom's world. Gatsby and Daisy leave in his huge yellow car and the others follow 'on toward death'. Nick's narrative uses the subsequent evidence of Michaelis at the inquest to fill in details of what happened at the garage before Myrtle Wilson rushed out to intercept the speeding yellow car.

Nick then resumes his own story of their arrival at the garage, where Myrtle is already dead and wrapped in a blanket.

Back at the Buchanan house, Nick sees Gatsby waiting alone for a pre-arranged signal from Daisy. He guesses that Daisy had been driving when Myrtle was killed. He looks into the house and sees Tom and Daisy sitting in an air of 'natural intimacy' over a plate of cold food, and he knows that Gatsby is waiting in vain – 'watching over nothing'.

Ch. VIII (pp. 140–54)   Nick recounts more of what Gatsby tells him that night of his wartime love affair with Daisy Fay. This is the third reference to it in the novel, and it completes the image of Gatsby's 'romantic readiness' mentioned at the beginning. Daisy was the only 'nice' girl Gatsby had known till then. After the war, demobbed and without prospects, he was effectively shut out of her opulent and exclusive world. Nick draws further on the evidence given by Michaelis at the subsequent inquest to recount what happened at Wilson's garage. He reconstructs in his imagination Gatsby's last moment of desolation following the destruction of his dream, as he lay in his swimming pool unaware that, like a spectre in the bitter new world of reality, 'that ashen, fantastic figure [was] gliding towards him through the amorphous trees'.

Fitzgerald thus keeps the three violent deaths out of the narrative. The effect in this chapter is to concentrate attention on Nick's sense of Gatsby's despair, which is expressed brilliantly by use of the nightmare imagery associated with the valley of ashes.

Ch. IX (pp. 155–72)   Nick's narrative returns to the present of his 'writing' the story with the words:

> 'After two years I remember the rest of that day, and that night and the next day, only as an endless drill of police and photographers and newspaper men in and out of Gatsby's front door.' (p. 155)

Fitzgerald thus eliminates all inessential details, placing the emphasis on Gatsby's isolation in death and his despair.

Nick is the only character at all interested in Gatsby after his death, and this effects a significant contrast with all the earlier gossip. Mr Henry C. Gatz from Minnesota arrives, but the old man's incomprehension only serves to isolate Gatsby further. At the funeral 'nobody came' until Owl-eyes arrives.

Nick's last act is to visit Gatsby's deserted mansion. After erasing an obscenity scrawled on the white steps, he wanders down to the shore and there, in his solitude, he experiences the moment of vision which draws together his own and Gatsby's acts of imaginative perception into a continuous flow of American history and all such individual attempts to find a transcendent beauty in life. He recognizes that 'reality' for any individual encompasses both a confrontation with the problems posed by history (that is, material time) and the exercise of a capacity for (timeless) creative acts of the imagination. By responding imaginatively to the total division of these two aspects of experience in Gatsby's life, Nick gives his own 'reality' a moral dimension which was missing in Gatsby.

THE SELECTIVE USE OF TIME AS A NARRATIVE DEVICE

By handling time in this complex way, Fitzgerald places the emphasis on Gatsby's emotions and on Nick's responses to them rather than on events. As a result, the past emerges less as a consecutive series of happenings than as a psychological drama within Gatsby's imagination. Fitzgerald reduces events in the summer of 1922 to a minimum for the same reason, and is thus able to draw Nick gradually into Gatsby's interior world. A good example of the very selective presentation of time occurs at the beginning of Chapter IV when Nick gives a list of Gatsby's guests that summer.

p. 60

> Once I wrote down on the empty spaces of a time-table the names of those who came to Gatsby's house that summer. It is an old time-table now, disintegrating at its folds, and headed 'This schedule in effect July 5th, 1922'. But I can still read the grey names, and they will give you a better impression than my generalities of those who accepted Gatsby's hospitality and paid him the subtle tribute of knowing nothing whatever about him.

Nick's irony at the expense of Gatsby's guests is deliberate, for his reference to their lack of interest in the host who is lavishing such generosity upon them acts as an indictment of their moral indifference. However, Nick's remark also highlights Gatsby's isolation and the vacuum in which his social identity exists. He is indeed Mr Nobody from Nowhere (p. 123). Nick's summary compresses a sequence of parties into a single general image; the 'grey names' are not merely recorded on paper already turning grey with age, they are morally 'grey', as Nick's account of their activities, leading in some cases to violent deaths, makes clear. The repetition of 'time-table' reinforces the idea of the inexorable ordering of time, despite the fact that the narrative keeps moving backward to the past which Gatsby is trying to re-create. Gatsby's desire to 'repeat the past' must inevitably be frustrated by time.

Just as time in the novel is carefully structured to create strands of an intricate pattern of meaning, the restriction of the locations serves a similar function. The four settings are put into significant relationships with each other through the perspectives which Nick, as narrator, provides. A brief examination of them will make this clear.

The relationship between the four locations of action

To take a very limited perspective, West Egg can be seen as representing vulgarity and formlessness, as opposed to the formality and style of East Egg. New York acts as a magnet to both those possessing established wealth and those eagerly in pursuit of it. All three locations are the product of the fabulous wealth that modern society creates. But such a precise fixing of their social status and identity in the historical context of the 1920s alone would limit their role and do no justice to Fitzgerald's handling of them. In the novel they are ambivalent locations which by the processes of Nick's imagination attain their own particular radiance, for his relationship with them constantly changes. They therefore exist in the novel as symbolic places representing the subjective moods at moments in time in Nick's or Gatsby's experience. Products of wealth themselves, some at least of their appeal to the observing eye of Nick or Gatsby exists in that wealth. Just as Gatsby's imagination transfigures his house into a place of enchantment, so Nick, a young man setting out to make his fortune, perceives them with the fresh, optimistic eyes of youthful hope. Yet in his role of narrator after the events of 1922 are over, he adds a note of moral awareness which marks him as receptive to the realities under the glittering surface. Nick's dual role of participant and subsequent narrator is an important factor in the representation of these locations.

WEST EGG

The area is dominated in the novel by Gatsby's magnificent, but somehow futile, baronial mansion. During his parties it is given a particular ambience which associates it with show-business people from Broadway and the world of films. The list of visitors 'who came to Gatsby's house that summer' (pp. 60–62) consists of names which are comic and yet suggestive too. There are those 'connected with the movies in one way or another' (p. 61), and 'theatrical people', and men accompanied by a whole array of girls whose 'last names were either the melodious names of flowers or months or the sterner ones of the great American capitalists whose cousins, if pressed, they would confess themselves to be' (p. 62). They are described at Gatsby's second party as 'on a short-cut from nothing to nothing' (p. 103) and the names listed are satirically suggestive. For example, the names of the Stonewall Jackson Abrams of Georgia and Mrs Ulysses Swett create deliberate reminders of Civil War heroes but imply the decline of America's heroic past. A number are implicated in violence: for instance there is the man called Snell who three days before he went to the penitentiary lay so drunk out on the gravel that Mrs Swett's car ran over his right hand. Among the movie moguls is 'G. Earl Muldoon, brother to that Muldoon who afterward strangled his wife'; from New York came Henry L. Palmetto 'who killed himself by jumping in front of a subway train in Times Square', and there is young Brewer 'who had his nose shot off in the war'. They all represent an energetic, careless and callous society which is breaking away from past moral and social restrictions. When she attends Gatsby's party, Daisy is appalled and offended by their noisy vulgarity and she fails to understand their vitality.

EAST EGG

By contrast East Egg observes the rules of formality and tradition, at least on the surface of life. The Buchanans' world is exclusive, opulent and self-regarding. It represents the status of inherited wealth and power to which the inhabitants of West Egg are denied access. The 'white palaces' glitter along the shoreline, but there is an implication that they are rather like whited sepulchres inhabited by people who are just as careless and socially indifferent as the ones who come to Gatsby's parties, but their inhabitants live with more style. Nick criticizes them at the end of the novel:

They are careless people, Tom and Daisy . . . they smashed up things and then retreated back into their money or their vast carelessness, or whatever it was that kept them together, and let other people clean up the mess they had made. (p. 170)

NEW YORK

New York lures all the characters, just as it initially drew Nick from the Midwest with 'Midas and Morgan and Maecenas' (p. 10) in mind as exemplars of the success he wants to achieve in stockbroking. Midas was a legendary king who turned everything he touched into gold; Maecenas was a very wealthy Roman; J. P. Morgan was a millionaire American financier in the nineteenth century. When Nick hurries 'down the white chasms [the skyscrapers] of lower New York to the Probity Trust' (pp. 56–7) he is in pursuit of such fabulous wealth as theirs. Yet New York also appeals to Nick in all its social variety and vitality. He enjoys

. . . the racy, adventurous feel of it at night, and the satisfaction that the constant flicker of men and women and machines gives to the restless eye. (p. 57)

He responds to the sense of romance in it

. . . at eight o'clock, when the dark lanes of the Forties were lined five deep with throbbing taxicabs, bound for the theatre district. (p. 57)

Nick's New York pulses with life. The city is filled with light and colour, for example on that 'almost pastoral' Sunday afternoon in Chapter II when 'the late afternoon sky bloomed in the window for a moment like the blue honey of the Mediterranean' (p. 36) or when the sunlight flickered upon the cars crossing the Queensboro Bridge (p. 67). Nick loves the soft summer twilights, and when he drives through Central Park with Jordan after she has told him of Gatsby's affair with Daisy, he is particularly aware of the beauty.

The sun had gone down behind the tall apartments of the movie stars in the West Fifties, and the clear voices of children, already gathered like crickets on the grass, rose through the hot twilight:

> '*I'm the Sheik of Araby.*
> *Your love belongs to me.*
> *At night when you're asleep*
> *Into your tent I'll creep.*' (p. 76)

The clear voices of the children suggest innocence, though the popular hit song of 1921 is morally ambivalent.

THE VALLEY OF ASHES

A landscape which serves as a grotesque symbol, the valley of ashes represents the grim underside of the other three: it is a part of all of them. The name given to it by Nick is reminiscent of the Psalmist's 'valley of the shadow of death', and the language describing it on p. 26 characterizes it as an obscene perversion of a fertile rural landscape. The road and railway 'shrink away from the fantastic farm where ashes grow like wheat into ridges and hills and grotesque gardens'. The men working on it raise 'an impenetrable cloud which screens their operations from your sight'. Wilson's garage stands on the edge of this wasteland 'and contiguous to absolutely nothing' (p. 27). Fitzgerald's use of the word 'nothing' links Wilson with Gatsby through a pattern of the words 'nobody', 'nowhere' and 'nothing'. In their very different ways they are both victims of society and they have no identity.

All four locations are later brought together, or superimposed upon each other, in the two nightmare landscapes existing within Nick's mind near the end of the novel: first in Nick's imagined reconstruction of the world which Gatsby's eyes looked at in his last moments, when he perceived a new reality in place of the dream that had dominated his life and discovered

what a grotesque thing a rose is and how raw the sunlight was upon the scarcely created grass (p. 153)

and second in Nick's own haunted vision, 'distorted beyond my eyes' power of correction' (p. 167). These landscapes are all linked through imagery, a feature of Fitzgerald's narrative representation which I shall consider next.

An examination of the recurrent images in *The Great Gatsby* makes clear the impossibility of isolating any particular one: they are inter-related in an intricate patterning of associations which contribute meaning to the central experience. They convey most effectively the beauty, transience and insubstantiality of Gatsby's dream, a world transfigured by imagination. The dream and the hope that goes into creating it are an illusion, yet the final vision of the novel, which employs many of the earlier images, gives them a value which sets them above the corrupt, the cruel or the meretricious features of society. The grand scale of Gatsby's belief 'in the green light, in the orgastic future' (p. 171), makes him a tragic figure. Yet Gatsby is also a paradoxical figure who is implicated fully in the corruption of the 1920s, and the novel is as ambivalent towards him as it is to New York: the tensions between reality or dream and illusion are central to the novel, and they are to be found chiefly in Nick's attitudes towards Gatsby and New York.

In his letter of 1937 already quoted in Chapter 1, Fitzgerald wrote of his desire to evoke a quality of 'hauntedness' in the novel. This might seem surprising in view of the presence of betrayal, corruption and violence on the one hand, and a strong element of social satire on the other. In addition, deception, self-deception and delusion are important features of the lives of all the characters. While Gatsby dreams on a grand scale, the others merely fantasize or construct some idea of themselves which suits their egotism. Nick is acutely aware of the incongruousness of their desires. For example, Daisy claims a fashionable world-weary pessimism; Tom Buchanan sees himself as the defender of the old-fashioned values of the family and the purity of women; Wolfshiem guards the honour of his mother and his sister by associating only with men of fine breeding. They all construct ideas of themselves which are at odds with the reality of their lives in a society permeated with individual delusions because it has lost all contact with values traditionally defining moral reality. Yet, as I have already suggested, Fitzgerald's style of writing attributes ambiguity, a dual quality dependent on the eyes perceiving them, to people and places, for example, to Daisy, to the young women at Gatsby's first party, to New York, to Gatsby's house. 'Reality' is always ambivalent, but is particularly so without the presence of a personal ethical awareness.

The word 'hauntedness' in Fitzgerald's letter of 1937 is difficult to define, and it suggests a range of association: death, ghosts, memory, the effects of someone or something on the imagination, dream, obsessive desire, illusion or the elusive aspects of emotional experience which defy precise definition. All of these associations form a part of Gatsby's story. To catch these qualities in the texture of his writing Fitzgerald created certain motifs, that is, meanings which are suggested by the recurrence of words and images. Some of these create ideas so powerfully that they function symbolically in the intricate patterning of the novel.

Patterns of imagery

DEATH AND GHOSTS

Most of Nick's early experiences in New York appear to be frivolous, banal or comic, yet the novel ends with the shattering of Gatsby's dream and Nick's own sense of disorientation as an onlooker upon betrayals and violent deaths. Daisy betrays Gatsby's faith by deserting him, and Tom betrays him to Wilson, justifying himself afterwards with the comment, 'That fellow had it coming to him' (p. 169). Yet the transition from comic to tragic is not sudden or unexpected, because Fitzgerald's language creates a series of images of death and ghosts operating as a sombre undertone from the start and sustaining the elegiac note on which the novel begins, when Gatsby is already spoken of by Nick in the past tense. At her dinner party in Chapter I Nick tells Daisy jokingly that she is so missed in Chicago that 'All the cars have the left rear wheel painted black as a mourning wreath, and there's a persistent wail all night along the north shore' (p. 15). After a dinner disturbed by tensions resulting from the telephone call to Tom, 'Tom and Miss Baker, with several feet of twilight between them, strolled back into the library, as if to a vigil beside a perfectly tangible body' (p. 21). The 'body' could be what is unspoken among them all as a result of the 'fifth guest's shrill metallic urgency' (p. 21), but the reference also insinuates a reminder of death into this elegant social occasion. At Myrtle's impromptu party in Chapter II she makes a great deal of fuss about the shopping she has to do, though really she is showing off her new consumer power as Tom's mistress. Among the things she has to buy is 'a wreath with a black silk bow for mother's grave that'll last all summer' (p. 38). Near the end of the novel, the violent impact of Gatsby's huge yellow car causes her to mingle 'her thick dark blood with the dust' (p. 131) and puts an end to her 'tremendous vitality' (p. 131) before the summer is over: what seems an ordinary wish at the beginning takes on ironic significance later. The same is true of her impatient sexual desire when she responded to Tom's arrogant sexuality earlier by telling herself: 'You can't live forever; you can't live forever' (p. 38).

In Chapter IV when Nick drives to New York with Gatsby, the huge vehicle 'scattered light through half Astoria' (p. 66), but the narration immediately moves from such light to death: 'A dead man passed us in a hearse heaped with blooms, followed by two carriages with drawn blinds, and by more cheerful friends' (p. 67). There are at least mourners here, whereas later at Gatsby's funeral, 'nobody came'. In Chapter V Gatsby himself is 'pale as death' (p. 83) when he presents himself at Nick's house a second time for tea with Daisy: he creates a comic figure here, 'standing in a puddle of water glaring tragically into my eyes' (p. 83), but the language associates him with death.

Closely linked with these images of death are those of ghosts, many focusing on Gatsby or his house. After his first party in Chapter III, as Nick and other guests gaze apprehensively at Owl-eyes and his car shorn 'violently' of one wheel, there is 'a ghostly pause' (p. 55) as another figure steps out of the car and the 'apparition' sways drunkenly. Again the situation is comic, but it associates motor cars with violence and potential death. In Chapter V, when Gatsby takes Daisy on a tour of his vast and silent house, as he closes the door of the 'Merton College Library' Nick fancies he hears 'the owl-eyed man break into ghostly laughter' (p. 88); later in Chapter VIII, as he keeps Gatsby company after the disastrous trip to New York, while fumbling for a light switch Nick 'tumbled with a sort of splash upon the keys of a ghostly piano' (p. 140). At the second party, one of the guests is a scarcely human 'orchid of a woman', a 'ghostly celebrity of the movies' (p. 101). At the end of Chapter V, when Nick recounts Gatsby's five-year dream of Daisy, he comments: 'No amount of fire or freshness can challenge what a man can store up in his ghostly heart' (p. 93). It is rather a strange expression to use of Gatsby's search for imaginative self-realization, and it perhaps makes an oblique reference to the creative fire of the Holy Ghost. However, such language reinforces the reader's sense of Gatsby's vulnerability in a society which has no place for creative imagination and in which Tom's brutal physique and social arrogance hold all the power. After Gatsby's second party – which is also his last – in Chapter VI, Nick glances up at the windows of the house.

Sometimes a shadow moved against a dressing-room blind above, gave way to another shadow, an indefinite procession of shadows, who rouged and powdered in an invisible glass. (pp. 103–4)

The guests are transformed into shadows, figures with no substance, just like ghosts. When in Chapter VII Nick realizes that Gatsby has closed his house to guests, and is told this is a way of maintaining the secrecy of Daisy's visits, he uses an image suggestive of an exotic Eastern scene, with implications perhaps of a mirage or something out of the Arabian Nights. A 'caravansary' is an Eastern inn at which merchants stopped for a night before moving on across the desert, just as Gatsby's guests drop in casually.

So the whole caravansary had fallen in like a card house at the disapproval in her eyes. (p. 109)

The unreality of Gatsby's dream, which he had transformed into a reality in his imagination, is summed up by Nick as he imagines the last moments of Gatsby's life after the disintegration of his dream, and with it his identity and his life.

A new world, material without being real, where poor ghosts, breathing dreams like air, drifted fortuitously about … (p. 154)

On a previous occasion, in Chapter IV, when Nick puts his arm around Jordan Baker, he draws her to him and kisses her. This contrasts with Gatsby's kiss when he centred all his dreams of the future on the figure of Daisy Fay in the moonlight. As he kisses Jordan, Daisy as an elusive dream is uppermost in Nick's mind, since Jordan has just been telling him of Gatsby's faithfulness to Daisy over the last five years, but he is aware of the difference.

Unlike Gatsby and Tom Buchanan, I had no girl whose disembodied face floated along the dark cornices and blinding signs, and so I drew up the girl beside me, tightening my arms. Her wan, scornful mouth smiled, and so I drew her up again closer, this time to my face. (p. 78)

Nick sees Gatsby as haunted by the mirage of Daisy that he invented.

Gatsby himself often seems as elusive or insubstantial as a ghost. As Nick gazes at him at the end of Chapter I, he glances out to sea to find out what is the object of his neighbour's intent look, and within that moment 'Gatsby had vanished' (p. 25). Similarly in Chapter IV, when Nick introduces him to Tom Buchanan in the restaurant, he turns back to draw Gatsby into the conversation only to find he was no longer there (p. 72). After the confrontation in the Plaza Hotel in Chapter VII, Tom contemptuously lets Daisy drive home with Gatsby:

'Go on. He won't annoy you. I think he realizes that his presumptuous little flirtation is over.' (p. 129)

Nick conveys the completeness of Gatsby's defeat:

They were gone, without a word, snapped out, made accidental, isolated, like ghosts, even from our pity. (p. 129)

Wilson is a ghost of a different kind. He is emotionally, economically and physically defeated by life, drained of vitality and identity. Like the 'ash-grey men' who swarm over the dustheaps nearby, creating crowds of grey dust, he is a grey man, 'blond, spiritless, anaemic' (p. 27). Tom says of him, 'He's so dumb he doesn't know he's alive' (p. 29). As a feature of this symbolic landscape, he isn't. Symbolically the dustheaps are linked with the 'foul dust that floated in the wake of his [Gatsby's] dreams' (p. 8); Wilson is the victim of a callous and indifferent society that casts the unsuccessful on to the rubbish dump of history. Myrtle Wilson is vital and full of sexual energy, but she too is drawn into the web of associative images of ghosts and dust. In Tom's flat the enlarged photograph of her mother on the wall seems comically lower-class when Nick mistakes it for 'a hen sitting on a blurred rock' (p. 31), before he manages to make out the beaming countenance of a stout old lady. However, later, he speaks of it as hovering 'like an ectoplasm on the wall' (p. 32) and it suddenly acquires the sinister connotations of a ghost casting a shadow over Myrtle Wilson. When she dies Myrtle literally surrenders to the dust as she 'mingled her thick dark blood with the dust' (p. 131). The next day when Nick is near the ashheaps in the train he sees 'little boys searching for dark spots in the dust' (p. 148).

CARS

Throughout the novel, references to cars associate them with restlessness and also with power in all its manifestations and finally with death. They are the new emblem of consumer power, as well as of destructiveness and violence in modern society. When Gatsby was a penniless young soldier, Daisy's house became for him a centre of romance and mystery, 'redolent of this year's motor cars and of dances whose flowers were scarcely withered' (p. 143). In Chapter IV Nick drives with Gatsby 'over the great bridge' into the sunlight (p. 67). Cars are seen as constructions of luxury and light, and romance too, when Nick feels excluded from the life enjoyed by couples in the 'throbbing taxicabs' (p. 57) lined five-deep taking them to the theatre. But in a significant conversation he has with Jordan Baker – whose name is an amalgam of two American makes of car – the car becomes a metaphor for the kind of imperviousness to other people that characterizes Tom and Daisy and other such 'careless people' who are insulated by their wealth from the reality of others' lives. On this occasion Jordan has just driven so close to a workman that the fender 'flicked a button' on his coat.

'You're a rotten driver,' I protested. 'Either you ought to be more careful, or you oughtn't to drive at all.'
'I am careful.'
'No, you're not.'
'Well, other people are,' she said lightly.
'What's that got to do with it?'
'They'll keep out of my way,' she insisted. 'It takes two to make an accident.'
'Suppose you met somebody just as careless as yourself.'
'I hope I never will,' she answered. 'I hate careless people. That's why I like you.' (p. 59)

Both of them know they are really talking about ethical standards in this seemingly trivial wrangle, and Jordan makes her position perfectly clear.

Jordan does no more than flick the workman's coat, but elsewhere cars 'rip' and destroy: Mrs Ulysses Swett's car runs over the right hand of the drunk on Gatsby's drive (p. 61); when Tom has an affair with the hotel chambermaid in Santa Barbara she is injured when he 'ran into a wagon on the Ventura road one night and ripped a front wheel off his car' (p. 75). After Myrtle Wilson is knocked down by Daisy, the men who run out see 'that her left breast was swinging loose like a flap, and there was no need to listen for the heart beneath. The mouth was wide open and ripped a little at the corners . . .' (p. 131). The language is repetitive in its insistence upon violence. The impersonal death machine violates Myrtle's female identity and ravages her: it is a symbolic rape. George Wilson deals in wrecks: 'the only car visible was a dust-covered wreck of a Ford which crouched down in a dim corner' (p. 27). Both Tom and Gatsby are responsible for the social chasm dividing Wilson from them and relegating him to a dim corner of society; their wealth and their cars brutally destroy him.

IMAGERY OF NATURE

Intermingled with these images of death are others serving as a reminder of natural beauty and transience, which in some ways make a contrast with them and in others reinforce their significance. Fitzgerald employs images of flowers and the seasons which are suggestive of the cyclical pattern of death and rebirth: images of moon and stars, sunlight and colour and birdsong pervade the novel, filling it with a sense of intense beauty, however evanescent this may be. Such beauty is often associated with the luxurious houses in the novel, serving as a reminder of the transforming power of wealth, but it also has particular reference to Daisy, attributing to her beauty a memorable quality which conveys how her memory haunts Gatsby.

Flowers

Daisy's name is itself a flower with distinctive white and gold colouring, and she herself is repeatedly associated with flowers through their colour and perfume. When Nick dines with the Buchanans in Chapter I he moves through 'a half-acre of deep pungent roses' (p. 13) before arriving at the 'rosy-coloured space' of the drawing-room. When he and Daisy rejoin Tom and Jordan after dinner, 'the crimson room bloomed with light' (p. 22). The word is repeated near the end of the novel when Gatsby keeps vigil outside Daisy's window, waiting for the signal he refuses to believe will not come; as Tom looks up at the house 'two windows bloomed with light among the vines' (p. 135). They bloom for Tom, not for Gatsby. The word picks up an earlier point in Nick's account of Gatsby's affair with Daisy in 1917, when he kissed her then and enshrined his ideal vision of her in his memory, and 'she blossomed for him like a flower and the incarnation was complete' (p. 107). On the ecstatic occasion of his reunion with her at Nick's tea-party in Chapter V, he takes her over to his house, visible symbol of his wealth, and his garden frames her with blossom and fragrance: she

admired the gardens, the sparkling odour of jonquils and the frothy odour of hawthorn and plum blossoms and the pale gold odour of kiss-me-at-the-gate. (p. 88)

Three years earlier when Daisy grew tired of waiting for Gatsby's return to Louisville from the war, she felt the pressures of her social world forcing her to resume her life as a beautiful débutante, and the imagery associates her with orchids, the most expensive of feminine corsages.

For Daisy was young and her artificial world was redolent of orchids and pleasant, cheerful snobbery and orchestras which set the rhythm of the year, summing up the sadness and suggestiveness of life in new tunes. (p. 143)

It was a world from which Gatsby was excluded by poverty.

... suddenly she was again keeping half a dozen dates a day with half a dozen men, and drowsing asleep at dawn with the beads and chiffon of an evening dress tangled among the dying orchids on the floor beside her bed. (p. 144)

When Fitzgerald uses the image of the orchid again it is in the context of Daisy's single visit to Gatsby's party, when the vulgar and frenetic vitality is not to her taste. Daisy approves of the famous film-star who sits frozen in an artificial pose all the evening: 'I like her, I think she's lovely' (p. 103). The star is 'a gorgeous, scarcely human orchid of a woman who sat in state under a white-plum tree' (p. 101). The connotations of wealth and the hothouse show both Daisy and the film-star to be cosseted, fragile blooms.

Birds

Daisy is also associated with the song of birds, her voice being the source of her sexual attraction which draws men to her. In Chapter I her voice exercises 'a singing compulsion' (pp. 14–15), it is 'glowing and singing' (p. 19); when she returns to the table after a tense and angry exchange with Tom about the telephone call, she glances at Nick and remarks, in her usual style of inconsequential whimsy which is a feature of her charm:

'I looked outdoors for a minute, and it's very romantic outdoors. There's a bird on the lawn that I think must be a nightingale come over on the Cunard or White Star Line. He's singing away, –' Her voice sang: 'It's romantic, isn't it, Tom?' (p. 20)

Her suggestion that the bird has come over from England on a luxury liner introduces an indirect reference to another nightingale in a summer, flower-filled garden, and the cadence of her voice is used to stress that association. Daisy is being identified by Fitzgerald with the nightingale in Keats's 'Ode to a Nightingale', in which the poet creates out of the bird's song an ecstatic moment that seems to transcend pain, death and time; such a transfiguring moment cannot last, and the song fades, leaving the poet to face the reality of harsh experience. In this way Gatsby's romantic vision of Daisy is given universal validity as an act of the creative imagination. When Nick first glimpses the distant figure of his neighbour gazing across at the green light it is 'a loud, bright night, with wings beating in the trees' (p. 25), and thus Gatsby too is drawn into this referential pattern of images.

Moonlight

Gatsby and his house are frequently associated with moonlight or star-light. In Chapter I Nick's first view of him is as a figure in the moonlight 'regarding the silver pepper of the stars' (p. 25); and at his first party his guests 'came and went like moths among the whisperings and the champagne and the stars' (p. 41). His enormous garden becomes a Christmas tree with coloured lights where he 'dispensed starlight to casual moths' (p. 76). When Nick first speaks to the polite stranger who turns out to be his host at the party, 'the moon had risen higher, and floating in the Sound was a triangle of silver scales, trembling a little to the stiff, tinny drip of the banjoes on the lawn' (p. 48). After the comic interlude of the owl-eyed man's drunken accident, Nick glances back at the house.

A wafer of a moon was shining over Gatsby's house, making the night fine as before, and surviving the laughter and the sound of his still glowing garden. A sudden emptiness seemed to flow now from the windows and the great doors, endowing with complete isolation the figure of the host, who stood on the porch, his hand up in a formal gesture of farewell. (p. 56)

Moonlight is traditionally associated with the romantic imagination, with an intense subjective experience of solitude, with reverie and desire for the unattainable ideal. Even in the heat and tension of Daisy's luncheon party in Chapter VII there is 'a silver curve of the moon [hovering] already in the western sky' (p. 114). Just before this, at the end of Chapter VI, in Nick's account of Gatsby's transfiguring emotion as he kissed Daisy five years earlier, 'the sidewalk was white with moonlight' (p. 106). When Gatsby keeps his futile vigil outside Daisy's window after the return from New York, Nick leaves him 'standing there in the moonlight – watching over nothing' (p. 139).

The golden sun

All the imagery of birdsong, starlight and moonlight conveys a particularly soft and muted radiance that is associated with a romantic or an idealizing emotion. Daisy, on the other hand, as the object of Gatsby's intense feeling, is associated more often with golden sunlight, but the gold, however, suggests hard, valuable metal too. Daisy and Jordan are not so distanced from the world of Dan Cody, who made his fortune through precious metals, as might at first seem to be the case. In Chapter I Tom's house glows 'with reflected gold' (p. 12) in Nick's eyes, and the drawing-room in which Nick finds Daisy is a 'rosy-coloured space' (p. 13). As they sit outside at dinner, Daisy winks 'ferociously toward the fervent sun' (p. 18) in mockery of Tom, and later 'the last sunshine fell with romantic affection upon her glowing face' ... 'then the glow faded, each light deserting her with lingering regret' (p. 19). When she arrives at Nick's bungalow for tea, 'two rows of brass buttons on her dress gleamed in the sunlight' (p. 87). Later, during her luncheon party in Chapter VII, when Gatsby defines the particular quality of Daisy's voice that constitutes her sexual charm he says, 'Her voice is full of money' (p. 115) and Nick searches for an imaginative image that sums up his companion's worship of her: 'the cymbal's song of it ... High in a white palace the king's daughter, the golden girl ...' (p. 115). In this image Daisy becomes the princess, cosseted and protected by wealth, drawing her allure from it and given value by her distance from ordinary mortals. Immediately after this, Daisy and Jordan, who, in a scene reminiscent of their first appearance in Chapter I, at first lay stretched on a couch 'like silver idols weighing down their own white dresses' (p. 110), later appear dressed for town, wearing small tight hats of metallic cloth (p. 115). When Gatsby recounts to Nick his passion for Daisy in 1917 his love for her is inextricably linked with her wealth (p. 142), and he was 'overwhelmingly aware of the youth and mystery that wealth imprisons and preserves, of the freshness of many clothes, and of Daisy, gleaming like silver ... and proud above the hot struggles of the poor' (p. 142). Daisy's charm and beauty are natural, but they are also the product of her upbringing and environment of great wealth. By his language Fitzgerald suggests a range of meanings which in turn create echoes of other meanings: for instance, in the same section of the narrative, Daisy's girlhood in Louisville, Kentucky, is evoked in a very rhythmical sentence ending with the word 'dust':

All night the saxophones wailed the hopeless comment of the 'Beale Street Blues' while a hundred pairs of golden and silver slippers shuffled the shining dust. (pp. 143–4)

The gold and silver slippers are the emblem of their wealth, but dust here acts as a reminder of the passing of time and the transience of youth, thus adding an elegiac quality in accord with blues music which is endorsed by Fitzgerald's prose cadences.

COLOUR

Fitzgerald uses colour to convey characteristic qualities or emotions. Daisy, like her flower name, is always linked with white as well as gold, so that there is always a dual association of innocence as well as wealth. Daisy is not innocent, but despite her worldliness she responds to Gatsby's romantic imagination, and the colour white creates a contrast to the implications of gold. On both occasions when Nick visits her house, she and Jordan seem at first to float or fly or balloon in their white dresses in the air-currents in the room (pp. 13, 110). When Jordan recalls her first meeting with Lieutenant Jay Gatsby, she describes Daisy as dressed in white and driving her little white roadster (p. 73). Daisy's looks are never described: an impressionist effect is achieved largely through the use of colour to suggest the impact of her beauty and sexuality on men. In Chapter IV when Nick gives his tea-party she arrives in her open car in the rain, and

Daisy's face, tipped sideways beneath a three-cornered lavender hat, looked out at me with a bright ecstatic smile . . . A damp streak of hair lay like a dash of blue paint across her cheek, and her hand was wet with glistening drops. (pp. 82–3)

The use of colour, the details of the streak of hair out of place and the glistening raindrops, give Daisy sexual vitality; she shows an awareness of beauty when she looks at the sunset creating a pink and golden billow of foaming clouds above the sea and whispers to Gatsby,

'I'd like just to get one of those pink clouds and put you on it and push you around.' (p. 91)

It is a rather inappropriate and banal remark, but at least it conveys a shared sense of the occasion.

Gatsby too is associated with colours, notably the green light which comes to symbolize the distant and unattainable Daisy of his vision.

Green is associated with life and growth. As he shows Daisy over his house, he refers to the green light, and Nick notes:

... he seemed absorbed in what he had just said. Possibly it had occurred to him that the colossal significance of that light had now vanished forever. Compared to the great distance that had separated him from Daisy it had seemed very near to her, almost touching her. It had seemed as close as a star to the moon. Now it was again a green light on a dock. His count of enchanted objects had diminished by one. (p. 90)

Just before this Gatsby has been tumbling his shirts out of the wardrobe for Daisy's inspection. Fitzgerald makes the banality of the situation intensely moving: Gatsby's ridiculous action is a reaction to his own tensions, but it is also a way of proving to Daisy the immense consumer power which he can command. The sensuousness and opulence of the materials is matched by the richness of the colours:

shirts with stripes and scrolls and plaids in coral and apple-green and lavender and faint orange, with monograms of indian blue. (p. 89)

Elsewhere, Gatsby's taste in colours denotes the vulgarity of the parvenu, at least in Tom's eyes:

'An Oxford man!' He was incredulous. 'Like hell he is! He wears a pink suit.' (p. 116)

Yet the colours of his suits are made to characterize his emotions. When he comes over to Nick's bungalow for the tea-party, his colour scheme echoes Daisy's attributes of white, silver and gold: 'Gatsby, in a white flannel suit, silver shirt, and gold-coloured tie, hurried in' (p. 81). On the day of the ill-fated trip to New York in Chapter VII he wears the pink suit that Tom objects to, but after his long vigil outside Daisy's window Nick notes:

His gorgeous pink rag of a suit made a bright spot of colour against the white steps. (p. 147)

When Gatsby's body is discovered by Nick and the servants, 'the laden mattress moved irregularly down the pool ...' (p. 154). Fitzgerald combines images of ritual or cyclical death and blood through the reference to the leaves which encircle it.

The touch of a cluster of leaves revolved it slowly, tracing, like the leg of transit, a thin red circle in the water. (p. 154)

The passage is given solemnity by the use of the image in place of direct reference to Gatsby's body.

EYES

The valley of ashes is linked with death in a number of ways. Even the oculist who set up the eyes of Doctor T. J. Eckleburg – his own name? – as a publicity stunt has now himself sunk into 'eternal blindness' (p. 26): the phrase 'solemn dumping ground' suggests a graveyard. However, it is the blind eyes which effect the most memorable image of a society existing in a moral vacuum, and the image becomes increasingly significant towards the end of the novel. When Nick, Tom and Jordan call at Wilson's garage on the way to New York in Chapter VII, 'the giant eyes of Doctor T. J. Eckleburg kept their vigil' (p. 118); after his wife's death Wilson tells Michaelis how he had warned his wife that she can't fool God, and Michaelis realizes with a shock that the God who 'sees everything' is Doctor T. J. Eckleburg.

'That's an advertisement,' Michaelis assured him. (p. 152)

Blindness and seeing operate as motifs in the novel, denoting the ability or the failure to perceive life in moral terms. The oculist who set the blind eyes over the dustheaps should have been engaged in correcting vision instead of seeking commercial advantage by means of a gimmick which is itself an image of materialism.

After Gatsby's death Nick is unable to perceive objectively, and dream and reality seem equally menacing as he 'tossed half-sick between grotesque reality and savage, frightening dreams' (p. 140); the East becomes a source of nightmare for him even though he knows that the nightmare and the dream are equally a distortion of the truth.

... the East was haunted for me like that, distorted beyond my eyes' power of correction. (p. 167)

Significantly, Owl-eyes makes a reappearance in the narrative as the only other mourner at Gatsby's funeral. As the comically drunk bespectacled guest at the first party, he was noted for his sense of surprise and wonder and his total oblivion to danger after the car crash. In Gatsby's library he made his insistent and triumphant discovery that the books, 'probably transported complete from some ruin' (p. 46) overseas, were real:

'See!' he cried triumphantly. 'It's a bona-fide piece of printed matter. It fooled me. This fella's a regular Belasco. It's a triumph. What thoroughness! What realism!' (p. 47)

David Belasco was a Broadway producer who created sets that looked real, and in his drunken awe the owl-eyed man puts his finger on the truth: Gatsby's way of life is a fantastic creation that he embarked upon to impress Daisy, but it is no more real than a stage production. In

Chapter IX, when Owl-eyes stands in the rain after Gatsby's funeral, he recognizes the nature of Gatsby's failure and expresses the only compassion in the novel.

> . . . 'Why, my God! they used to go there by the hundreds!'
> He took off his glasses and wiped them again, outside and in.
> 'The poor son-of-a-bitch,' he said. (p. 166)

He sees a moral truth without optical aid.

CLOCKS

Time is an important feature of Gatsby's story and, as it has already been suggested, the structure of the novel gives it significance. Gatsby is seen against a perspective of inexorable time by references to clocks at several points. During Nick's tea-party in Chapter V, Gatsby is comically distraught and gauche at first: he tilts his head so far back that he tips a 'defunct clock' on the mantelpiece and just manages to catch it. Nick adds, 'I think we all believed for a moment that it had smashed in pieces on the floor' (p. 84). Gatsby only *seems* to have pushed time backwards and destroyed its power. During the afternoon he is described as 'running down like an overwound clock' (p. 89). In Chapter VI when Nick recounts Gatsby's life as a seventeen-year-old drifter, he says, 'his heart was in a constant turbulent riot', and while he constructed dreams of fantastic wealth in his imagination 'the clock ticked on the washstand and the moon soaked with wet light his tangled clothes upon the floor' (p. 95). The reality of 'clock' time is placed in opposition to the moonlight of romantic possibilities very deliberately in this passage – fantastic dreams must succumb to it, for time is history.

THE SEA

One of the most pervasive images in the novel concerns the sea. A source of life, it is by tradition often linked metaphorically with the voyage as a form of emotional experience leading to maturity and moral awareness or recognition of one's true identity. There are many such voyages in literature. In *The Great Gatsby* a cluster of sea images imply perspectives of moral experience. In the opening section Nick speaks of

> What preyed on Gatsby, what foul dust floated in the wake of his dreams (p. 8)

– thus opposing dust, with its concomitant association of death or corruption, to Gatsby's act of creative imagination. Nick's final vision of the Dutch sailors links the sea-voyage of hope with the reality of history. Just before this he applies the oppositional relationship of sea and refuse to his own moral position. Before leaving New York he feels morally bound to end his affair with Jordan Baker rather than just going without a word: it is 'an awkward, unpleasant' thing to have to do:

> But I wanted to leave things in order and not just trust that obliging and indifferent sea to sweep my refuse away. (p. 168)

The reference is presumably to the purifying or cleansing function of time. After the horrors of the day in New York and Myrtle Wilson's death, as Nick lies tossing in tormented sleep, 'A fog-horn was groaning incessantly on the Sound' (p. 140); the fog represents his own confused and disturbed state of mind. At the beginning of that occasion, just before they have lunch, Fitzgerald uses the image of a sailing boat as a deliberate contrast to the mounting tension which they are all aware of:

> On the green Sound, stagnant in the heat, one small sail crawled slowly toward the fresher sea . . .
> Our eyes lifted over the rose-beds and the hot lawn and the weedy refuse of the dog-days alongshore. Slowly the white wings of the boat moved against the blue cool limit of the sky. Ahead lay the scalloped ocean and the abounding blessed isles. (pp. 112–13)

It is an extended image. First the colours green, blue and white amplify the idea of a 'fresher' world beyond the refuse on the shore. The solitude of 'one small sail' conveys an escape to isolation and peace, and it contrasts with the suppressed tensions within the group already exacerbated by the oppressive heat. The language and rhythm of the last sentence complete the sense of escape: 'scalloped' suggests the mysterious beauty of shells and also gives a certain unreality to the scene by likening the waves to the embroidered curves of scallop stitching.[2] All of them are investing the scene with the intensity of their own desire to escape the unpleasantness of their situation by discovering the abounding blessed isles of peace and thus to attain the new world of every voyager's quest.

The image perhaps prefigures Gatsby's lonely death floating on his pool mattress; the blessed isles are also often death, the final release.

Imagery gives the novel its particular tone. It allows Fitzgerald to move between sharp social observation and comedy of manners on the one hand and symbolic landscape on the other without any sense of strain or a break in the narrative. The novel is concerned with the individual's capacity to construct an idealizing vision in a blindly callous society given over to materialism. By means of the intricate patterning of images Fitzgerald is able to keep both these perspectives in a state of tension by focusing them on the personalities of Gatsby and Nick.

3. Alternative Worlds [1]

Fitzgerald has sometimes been accused of exaggerating the glamour of the lives of the rich and giving them a spurious attractiveness. The claim of the narrator of 'The Rich Boy', a short story dating from much the same period as *The Great Gatsby*, that 'The rich are different from you and me. They possess and enjoy early, and it does something to them' [2] expresses the source of Fitzgerald's own interest. It is not the rich themselves who are glamorized in his fiction so much as their spending power: they are defined by fashion, by the sensuousness and colour of their clothes, by the opulence of their homes and their cars and the freedom of their entertainments. In addition, the secure knowledge of great wealth frees them from the moral constraints to which the less well-endowed are subject.

In *The Great Gatsby* the Buchanans are framed by their luxurious house, and provided with a setting in which to receive their guests. Ultimately they can retreat into it at the first sign of trouble. Gatsby too is able to adopt a pose in his huge mansion as host to the multitudes who crowd his gardens and pay him 'the subtle tribute of knowing nothing whatever about him' (p. 60). Fitzgerald makes sharp discriminations between the two houses, however, not only through the relative social status of East and West Egg, signifying the gulf between the Buchanans' patrician position and Gatsby's parvenu wealth, but also through the language in which they are presented. These two houses, as well as Daisy's home in Louisville and the flat on 158th Street where Myrtle acts the lady of the house, are a means by which Fitzgerald represents their owners' emotions and self-images. In addition, like the valley of ashes they symbolize universals in modern society. In this chapter I shall begin by making a detailed study of the language and imagery in a number of passages representing their ways of life and the houses which express their identities.

The Buchanans' glittering white palace

pp. 12–13 The 'Georgian Colonial' style of the mansion asserts the Buchanans' place in American history: the style is imitation but it puts them among the élite and patrician, the established rich whose fortunes were made in an earlier generation. The description of the gardens conveys vitality and assertiveness, as if the extensive grounds are identified with their owner, Tom. The 'reflected gold' carries the double implication of sunshine and wealth. The paragraph ends with the picture of Tom Buchanan in the traditional pose of the man in possession.

> The lawn started at the beach and ran towards the front door for a quarter of a mile, jumping over sundials and brick walls and burning gardens – finally when it reached the house drifting up the side in bright vines as though from the momentum of its run. The front was broken by a line of french windows, glowing now with reflected gold and wide open to the warm windy afternoon, and Tom Buchanan in riding clothes was standing with his legs apart on the front porch.

The imagery of movement is suggestively masculine. It contrasts strongly with the drawing-room where the two women wait, poised and certainly posed, to receive their guest, once he has taken in the vision of Tom's property, which includes a 'sunken Italian garden, a half-acre of deep pungent roses and the motor-boat moored at the dock'.

Within the seemingly fragile 'bright rosy-coloured space' of the many-windowed drawing-room, the chief impression is of colours and movement which seem to effect a transformation: the curtains become flags and the play of shadows on the crimson rug becomes the rippling surface of the sea. The point of stillness to which the guest's eyes are drawn in the room is the huge couch which seems to be anchored amid the rippling sea, while the two young women in their white dresses are like fluttering sea-birds 'blown back in after a short flight around the house'. The effect so far has been of beauty, yet a new note is introduced as Nick stands listening to 'the whip and snap of the curtains and the groan of a picture on the wall': the language conveying the infliction of pain is a prelude to the 'boom' as Tom Buchanan exercises male mastery by shutting the windows and bringing the two young women ballooning down as their flimsy dresses stop fluttering in the breeze.

The description makes the room a place of enchantment: it acknowledges that money can command beauty and create an excitement of the senses. The scene fills Nick Carraway with a sense of wonderment by appealing to his imagination, and the two women in the room act deliberately to sustain his wonderment: they are entranced, transformed into strange, mysterious, magical creatures. Their passive femininity and allure show to advantage beside Tom's masculine bulk and assertion. The whole scene which they present to their guests is beautifully contrived. The rosy-coloured porch where dinner is later served further enhances Daisy's beauty, and she quickly snuffs out the candles whose artificial light would compete with her natural radiance. After dinner, when the four come together again, 'the crimson room bloomed with light' and the light picks out the golden colour of Jordan's hair. The colours are warm and muted. Their house is full of reflected light: brilliant gold sunshine, rosy sunset, candlelight and lamplight create different effects in which the women's beauty is shown off and their wealth is also reflected.

The Buchanans' surroundings are carefully contrived to impress their guest with the brilliance of the setting in which they, the possessors, shine in the particular roles they have adopted. Yet the passage is a *tour de force* on Fitzgerald's part. In showing how wealth can transform the ordinary, he is exploiting the transforming power of language and art and so enacting the theme of Gatsby's story – the transforming power of the imagination. The passage is a brilliant introduction to the major preoccupation of the novel. Reality and unreality are brought together in this opening section, and it is difficult for us as readers to disentangle and synthesize them in the total effect.

p. 110 In Chapter VII Nick makes no mention of the gardens during his second visit to the Buchanans' house, which forms the prelude to the catastrophe of death and betrayal. The wind from the fans blows towards him the faint sound of a telephone call, which turns out to be for Tom from Wilson, and this creates a pattern of repetition of the previous occasion. So too does the description of the two women, although this time the room creates no association with enchantment or magical transformation; it is darkened and the breeze is artificial.

The room, shadowed well with awnings, was dark and cool. Daisy and Jordan lay upon an enormous couch, like silver idols weighing down their own white dresses against the singing breezes of the fans.

The reference to idols identifies them as objects of worship but suggests a connection with wealth too. They are no longer the airy creatures of flight and weightlessness who presented themselves to Nick's awed gaze on his first visit. The reason is that Nick's perceptions have changed: he is less naïve and less easily impressed.

pp. 135 and 138 When Nick, Jordan and Tom return to the house after Myrtle Wilson's death, Daisy is already at home. The house 'floats' towards them through the trees and her bedroom windows 'bloomed with light'. The Buchanans' way of life is unchanged: in her beauty Daisy continues to blossom like a flower, and Tom's wealth can still command the aids to magic and enchantment. Nick's final description of them sets them in the pantry, seated at a table with cold chicken and ale before them. These are untouched, but the implications of their callous materialism are clear. Nick is actually spying on them, catching them unawares as he looks through a tear in the blind, and so they are no longer posed for the gaze of guests. The magic is gone, but they are secure, they are protected by their home, while Nick and Gatsby are outside, Nick because he has chosen to ally himself in this way, and Gatsby because he is excluded. There is a hint of collusion between husband and wife, a closing of ranks in terms of their caste. The reestablishment of their old relationship is signified by Tom's protective gesture and the way Daisy looks up at him, nodding occasionally in agreement. Tom has retained his possession of Daisy and has reestablished his supremacy.

Daisy's home in Louisville, Kentucky: the 'white palace' of the 'golden girl' (pp. 115 and 141–2)

Nick uses the phrase 'High in a white palace the King's daughter, the golden girl' (p. 115) as a metaphor which invokes a typical situation from fairy tales of the inaccessible high-born maiden and the poor suitor. It is usually her inaccessibility which gives her value in such stories. Gatsby's love for Daisy is associated with the house she lives in and takes for granted. The house itself as material object is of no importance in the novel, it is Gatsby's imaginative response to it that matters. In 1917 as a poor young officer who was out of his own class and who gained admittance only because of his uniform, he imagined unseen rooms, 'bedrooms upstairs more beautiful and cool than other bedrooms', the fund of pleasure to be found there, and love affairs redolent of the newest fashions in gleaming motor cars. He invests the house – and Daisy in it – with his imagination and attributes to it a quality of radiance in terms of youth and mystery which only wealth can sustain.

> Gatsby was overwhelmingly aware of the youth and mystery that wealth imprisons and preserves, of the freshness of many clothes, and of Daisy, gleaming like silver, safe and proud above the hot struggles of the poor. (p. 142)

He therefore perceives wealth as a source of power, not the mere social power that Tom Buchanan delights in, but the power to transcend the mundane and the reality of time and decay. Daisy and her home are inextricably linked with youth and power in Gatsby's dream – even her porch was bright with the 'bought luxury of star-shine' – but Gatsby attributes to them the radiance of the ideal. He transforms and makes enchanted the prosaic and the ordinary by an act of his imagination.

Gatsby's house

GATSBY'S FIRST PARTY IN EARLY SUMMER (pp. 41–56)

The opening of Chapter III matches the tone of the description of the Buchanans' house in Chapter I in achieving the transformation of materiality into a magical world. It depicts a scene of hedonism and plenty transformed into the enchanted at Gatsby's command. Ownership of this world is insisted upon by the repetition of 'his'.

There was music from my neighbour's house through the summer nights. In *his* blue gardens men and girls came and went like moths among the whispering and the champagne and the stars. At high tide in the afternoon I watched *his* guests diving from the tower of *his* raft, or taking the sun on the hot sand of *his* beach while *his* two motor-boats slit the waters of the Sound, drawing aquaplanes over cataracts of foam. On week-ends *his* Rolls-Royce became an omnibus, bearing parties to and from the city between nine in the morning and long past midnight, while *his* station wagon scampered like a brisk yellow bug to meet all trains. (p. 41) (italics mine)
... On buffet tables, garnished with glistening hors-d'oeuvre, spiced baked hams crowded against salads of harlequin designs and pastry pigs and turkeys bewitched to a dark gold ... (p. 41)

The lights grow brighter as the earth lurches away from the sun, and now the orchestra is playing yellow cocktail music ... the sea-change of faces and voices and colour under the constantly changing light. (p. 42)

The sense of a radiant, enchanted world is, however, undercut by Nick's comment on the guests who simply turn up uninvited and behave 'according to the rules of behaviour associated with an amusement park'. It is a kind of Coney Island: the scene is garish and the noise raucous. The style of writing gives it these double attributes: for the garden is at once magical and light-enchanted and it is a fairground, depending on the eyes viewing it. A fairground can be a vulgar place or it can be a place of enchantment. Perception of reality can be very much a matter of point of view.

The effect of this description is impressionistic: all the details signify undifferentiated, kaleidoscopic movement and colour and mood, rather than portraying individuals engaged in particular pleasures. The colours of 'blue gardens' or 'yellow cocktail music' convey the harmony of a summer scene at night under the glow of the stars and youth and happiness. Laughter is '*spilled* with prodigality', '*tipped* out at a cheerful word', and groups '*dissolve* and form in the same *breath*' [Italics mine]. The solid world of human bodies is transformed into the insubstantiality of Gatsby's dream by Fitzgerald's use of language. This impressionistic scene of movement and change creates a contrast with the solitary figure

55

of the host, and, although the reader is not yet aware of this, it anticipates the revelation of the essential insubstantiality of Gatsby's life which is to become increasingly evident. Initially, then, Gatsby's house is represented by his garden, which is at once mysteriously beautiful and a scene of 'spectroscopic gaiety' like a funfair. Thus Fitzgerald creates in such scenes a sense of the unreality of reality which Gatsby himself is to experience tragically later, while, after Gatsby's death, Nick in his troubled dreams is unable to distinguish between the two.

THE HISTORY OF GATSBY'S HOUSE

pp. 11 and 85–6 The description and history of Gatsby's house have significance in relation to its present owner. Initially Nick describes his neighbour's house as 'a colossal affair by any standard – it was a factual imitation of some Hôtel de Ville in Normandy'. An *hôtel de ville* in France is a public, institutional building, the mayor's office, and so at once Gatsby's house is presented as an edifice rather than a home that is given identity by those living in it. It is also an imitation. It is 'spanking new', and the attempt to make it ivy-clad – and therefore venerable with age – is made to seem spurious and a failure by the phrase 'a thick beard of ivy'. The marble swimming pool and the forty acres of ground impress Nick, as they are intended to impress Daisy. When Jordan first broaches the matter of the tea-party, she explains:

'He wants her to see his house'. (p. 77)

The central role of Gatsby's house in his dream of Daisy becomes increasingly clear: it has to prove to her that he has attained her exclusive world of great wealth and now has a 'real right to touch her hand' (p. 142). Yet the details of its brief history undermine this before the reader is aware of Gatsby's dream and associate it with failure, and later with death. There is a social gulf between West Egg, whose inhabitants are 'herded ... along a short-cut from nothing to nothing' (p. 103), and exclusive East Egg. Nick relates in the middle of Gatsby's ecstatic reunion with Daisy – again undermining the mood of triumph and happiness – that a brewer had built it ten years earlier, and in his attempt to set up a dynasty had cherished the notion of creating a feudal estate, which entailed the locals thatching their roofs. He had even tried to bribe them with the payment of their rates for five years, but to no avail. His dream was short-lived, and he died soon afterwards. His children showed their contempt for his aspiration by selling the house while the black wreath was still on the door: this detail anticipates the similar lack of concern for Gatsby once he is dead. Nick's comment about the cottages is ironic:

Americans, while willing, even eager, to be serfs have always been obstinate about being peasantry. (p. 86)

His discrimination passes an ironic judgement on American society: a serf is owned by his master, whereas a peasant has a level of independence in the social structure.

Gatsby's house is thus depicted through a double perspective. It is initially a centre of gaiety, a place rendered enchanted through an act of the imagination (both Gatsby's and Nick's). But at the same time the reality of history invokes a sense of failure and death. As observer and narrator Nick combines and balances both these modes of perceiving life. For instance, in the middle of the description on p. 41 of a hedonistic and transfigured world, he inserts a reminder of the actual work required of servants to achieve such effects.

... and on Mondays eight servants, including an extra gardener, toiled all day with mops and scrubbing brushes and hammers and garden-shears, repairing the ravages of the night before.

Every Friday five crates of oranges and lemons arrived from a fruiterer in New York – every Monday these same oranges and lemons left his back door in a pyramid of pulpless halves. There was a machine in the kitchen which could extract the juice of two hundred oranges in half an hour if a little button was pressed two hundred times by a butler's thumb. (p. 41)

The reality of the servants' lives is there for anyone who wants to include it in his awareness. Later, when Nick tactfully absents himself at his tea-party, he is aware of the servants in his neighbour's house whose lives constitute a presence which is given no recognition in Gatsby's dream. A grocer's van delivers 'the raw material' for their dinner – Gatsby will be too carried away by his ecstasy to eat. A maid opens the windows of his house, and 'leaning from the central bay', spits meditatively into the garden. The clarity of Nick's perception of the bored maid, carefully inserted into accounts of Gatsby's romantic emotion, offers an additional perspective of reality, making it more comprehensive than Gatsby's.

'SILENCE HAD FALLEN WITHIN THE HOUSE' (pp. 88–9)
When Gatsby takes Daisy on a tour of his house after Nick's tea-party in Chapter V, the description emphasizes the silence and then the pretentiousness of the building; the house seems fatuous because it is unused. It has never been lived in as a home, which might have given it some validity by associating it with people's daily lives. Architecturally the house is a jumble of styles: it claims to be a part of history, but like Gatsby, it is spurious.

And inside, as we wandered through Marie Antoinette music-rooms and

Restoration Salons, I felt that there were guests concealed behind every couch and table, under orders to be breathlessly silent until we had passed through. As Gatsby closed the door of 'the Merton College Library' I could have sworn I heard the owl-eyed man break into ghostly laughter.

We went upstairs, through period bedrooms swathed in rose and lavender silk and vivid with new flowers, through dressing-rooms and poolrooms, and bathrooms with sunken baths ...

The plural nouns emphasize the uselessness and ostentation of Gatsby's splendour. His boarder, the hungry Mr Klipspringer who sponges off him, is the only other occupant, and this makes clear the isolation of the owner. What Gatsby has to show Daisy are material possessions, including a toilet set of dull gold and shirts which proclaim his consumer power stretching right to the best tailors in England. He judges the value of everything by 'the measure of response it drew from her well-loved eyes'. It has no other meaning for him. Gatsby is no materialist, even though he needs material accumulation to express his dream and to prove himself worthy of Daisy.

Fitzgerald never defines exactly how Gatsby accumulated such a fabulous fortune: instead he puts the emphasis on his emotional state, because his wealth has no reality for him apart from Daisy's approval.

... he stared at his possessions in a dazed way, as though in her actual and astounding presence none of it was any longer real. (p. 88)

GATSBY'S LAST PARTY (pp. 100–107)
The 'scarcely human orchid of a woman' who sits in state under a white-plum tree would have been totally out of place at the earlier party. Now her presence adds to the sense of unease that Nick experiences, for he is looking through Daisy's eyes:

It is invariably saddening to look through new eyes at things upon which you have expended your own powers of adjustment.

Nick's emotional experience is increasingly identified with Gatsby's now that he is moving emotionally closer to him, and this is precisely what Gatsby himself is doing during his last party – looking through Daisy's eyes at the world he has created. The guests are there in their 'sparkling hundreds', but, viewed in terms of Daisy's social attitudes, they are raucous and drunk like Miss Baedeker and her friends, or 'massive and lethargic' like the woman who wants Daisy to play golf with her. It is Daisy's voice which now 'tipped out a little of her warm magic upon the air'; the word 'tipped' echoes the phrase used of the earlier party (p. 42), but now no one can compete with Daisy in Gatsby's world. Nick waits until the guests have gone, and by then the beach is 'black' and the lights are extinguished in the guest-rooms. As Gatsby confides to Nick the anticipated climax of his dream, which is nothing less than that Daisy should renounce five years of her life and 'go back to Louisville and be married from her house – just as if it were five years ago', he is walking up and down among the débris of the party:

. . . a desolate path of fruit rinds and discarded favours and crushed flowers.

The distortion of earlier images is deliberate, signifying the insubstantiality of his dream just as much as the fact that 'the lights in his house failed to go on one Saturday night' (p. 108). Gatsby's career as Trimalchio,[3] provider of all this 'spectroscopic gaiety', is over.

The introduction of Wolfshiem's protégés (p. 154) into the house once Gatsby closes it to guests both signals the end of his romantic optimism and acts as a reminder of the corruption which is the source of his wealth.

THE SWIMMING POOL (pp. 153–4)

Language and the use of detail consistently link Gatsby's house with darkness and emptiness, once the high emotional peak of his reunion with Daisy is past. His lonely death in his magnificent marble swimming pool is a climax that Fitzgerald's style of writing has anticipated. Nick imagines Gatsby's last moments when he has to face reality, including the final reality of the ghost figure of Wilson gliding towards him with a gun. (In Nick's reconstruction of the scene Gatsby is unaware of this.) Nick thinks he must have

looked up at an unfamiliar sky, through frightening leaves and shivered as he found what a grotesque thing a rose is and how raw the sunlight was upon the scarcely created grass.

The very ordinary presence of sky, leaves, rose and grass cannot be transfigured by his imagination now, and consequently their reality is like a nightmare for Gatsby in his final despair at the failure and destruction of his magnificent dream.

The visual detail of Gatsby's corpse is made memorable both by the rhythms of the sentences and by the way in which the images echo earlier ones. In fact, the body is not mentioned, which again constitutes a *tour de force* on Fitzgerald's part. This is the scene that meets Nick's eyes:

There was a faint, barely perceptible movement of the water as the fresh flow from one end urged its way toward the drain at the other. With little ripples that were hardly the shadows of waves, the laden mattress moved irregularly down the pool. A small gust of wind that scarcely corrugated the surface was enough to disturb its accidental course with its accidental burden. The touch of a cluster of leaves revolved it slowly, tracing, like the leg of transit, a thin red circle in the water.

Rippling waves and shadows and the small gust of wind now emphasize the patterns of alternating stillness and movement that recur through the novel right from the start in Daisy's drawing-room. The whole paragraph directs the reader's attention forwards to the final reference to the 'thin red circle in the water' – leaves, not blood. Gatsby's body is an 'accidental burden' on the rippling water. The reality of his death is made clear by the indirect reference to blood, but dead Gatsby is as distanced from the reader as he was when alive. The scene is transformed, transfigured by rhythm and imagery and by the absence of detail. The mode of writing continues to transform the material into the mysterious, and Gatsby's body becomes a sacrificial victim floating on the water. The falling autumnal leaves complete the suggestion of the cyclical passage of the season through the early summer of bloom and hope to the autumn of death.

'IT WAS A PHOTOGRAPH OF THE HOUSE' (p. 163)

After Gatsby's death, Mr Gatz's pride in his son and his son's possessions increases as he takes in the splendours of the house. Until this time he has known it only indirectly through the photograph 'cracked in the corners and dirty with many hands' which he has cherished as an emblem of his son's success. Nick realizes that the photograph is more real to him than the house itself, just as Gatsby's dream of achieving Daisy's acceptance of him by means of his possessions is more real to him than the possessions themselves. Mr Gatz's response endorses the popular conception of success, but it is made to convey to the reader the insubstantiality of Gatsby's dream. Nick's vision at the end of the novel achieves the same end by restoring the trees that had been cut down to make way for Gatsby's house. The grandiose building in all its futility is removed by a trick of his imagination, to be replaced by a vision of the Dutch sailors catching their breath at the beauty of what can only be an impossible dream of an ideal new life in a new land. By implication they are linked to Gatsby and to Nick himself as dreamers.

'A HUGE INCOHERENT FAILURE OF A HOUSE' (p. 171)

With this phrase, Nick defines the futility of Gatsby's dream in terms of his baronial house. The shoreline is dark now that the Long Island Summer residences are closed for winter:

... there were hardly any lights except the shadowy moving glow of a ferry boat across the Sound.

The green light on Daisy's dock has no significance now, for Gatsby is dead, but it is important to note that Nick's perception of the scene now encompasses a distant glow out on the water. The ferry boat is going about its mundane job of transporting ordinary people between the city and the island, but it is perceived as a mysterious distant radiance out on the ocean.[4] Nick achieves what Gatsby never did, a synthesis of the ordinary and the romantic: he recognizes that reality comprehends both what has material and objective existence in time and what is subjectively created by the idealizing imagination. Nick does not define such a recognition and may not be aware of it, but Fitzgerald's organization of the scene offers such an interpretation to the reader. Nick's trivial act of perceiving the ferry boat precedes his climactic vision which enacts a further synthesis of ways of seeing. 'Reality' without any imaginative glow of passion and characterized by moral indifference produces a valley of ashes of alienation: on the other hand, the 'dream' cherished without any awareness of history and its moral complexity is insubstantial, and the contemporary world, in particular, makes it very difficult for the individual to achieve such a balance. Gatsby certainly failed.

Plaza suite (pp. 119–29)

Fitzgerald needed to bring all his characters together for the catastrophe, and he succeeds brilliantly through the ghastly joy-ride in the intense heat of midday and the subsequent return home 'toward death through the twilight' in Chapter VII.

'What'll we do with ourselves this afternoon,' cried Daisy, 'and the day after that, and the next thirty years?' (p. 113)

She sounds very like the bored rich woman in the second section of T. S. Eliot's poem, *The Waste Land*.[5]

'But it's so hot,' insisted Daisy, on the verge of tears, 'and everything's so confused. Let's all go to town.' (p. 113)

The luxurious New York hotel affords them 'a place to have a mint julep' made with the whisky Tom has brought along; it was that or the unlikely alternative of hiring five cold baths. After prolonged argument they 'herd' into the hotel, and are consequently brought into close proximity in the stifling heat. The 'portentous chords of Mendelssohn's Wedding March from the ballroom below' serve to create an ironic contrast with the Buchanans' marriage, which began with 'pomp and circumstance' (p. 74) three years earlier but now seems to be on the point of breaking up. The wedding below acts ironically as a reminder of pledges made and hopes just beginning. However, the music prompts Tom and Daisy to reminisce with Jordan about their own wedding in a way that effectively excludes Gatsby as a social outsider who was formerly barred from their élite world of privately hired railway coaches. The musical shift from classical to jazz serves to increase the strain and tension among the five characters. Just at the point when Daisy begins to waver and Tom to assert his sexual and social dominance, the noisy, rhythmic music erupts into the scene to intensify the sense of claustrophobia and heat generated by the room.

The flat on 158th Street (pp. 31–9)

The flat Tom Buchanan rents for his clandestine affair with Myrtle Wilson is very different from his Long Island home, and it too conveys by implication the value he attributes to her. The repetitions in Nick's description emphasize how constricted it is: 'a small living-room, a small dining-room, a small bedroom, and a bath'. The suite of big tapestried furniture depicting 'ladies swinging in the gardens of Versailles' which is crowded into the living-room is both ridiculous and inappropriate in this setting. It suggests tastelessness and pretentiousness. The over-enlarged photograph of Myrtle's mother looking like a hen roosting on a rock, and the evidence of Myrtle's taste in reading, are a further indication: *Town Tattle* was a scandal magazine, and *Simon Called Peter* was a popular novel of 1921 of which Fitzgerald strongly disapproved. When Nick waits discreetly while Tom and Myrtle make love in the bedroom he judges the novel 'terrible stuff'. With her change of dress and the arrival of her guests Myrtle essays to adopt the manner of a society hostess, and she clearly wishes to assert her spending power. When Tom, who has already 'tanked up a good deal at luncheon' (p. 27), gives vent to his brutality and frustration by smashing Myrtle's nose with 'a short left movement', her precious furniture is her first concern. As Mrs McKee and Catherine stumble 'here and there among the crowded furniture', Myrtle, even though she is bleeding profusely, tries desperately to protect the tapestried scene from the blood. Tom's boredom and arrogant sense of his own superiority are evident in the way he has conducted himself throughout the scene.

  The really incongruous element in this tiny smoke-filled room crowded with self-absorbed people is the little dog, which by the end of the evening is left sitting on the table looking with blind eyes through the smoke, and from time to time groaning faintly.

The 'blind eyes' are a realistic detail, no doubt, but they function as a reference to the moral blindness pervading the novel: this is no place for the helpless. Myrtle's whim to improve her status among the property-owning classes required that Tom should buy her a dog as they were leaving the station:

'I want to get one for the apartment. They're nice to have – a dog.' (p. 29)

The little mongrel dog proffered by the street vendor, 'a grey old man who bore an absurd resemblance to John D. Rockefeller', one of the original millionaires in oil, is a pathetic product of the urban wasteland. The old man's sales technique is made to seem comic in this context, but it is noticeable that he adapts the price to Tom's evident affluence. The tiny creature is not exactly the police dog that Myrtle wants, but he assures her that it will never bother her by catching cold. When Myrtle coyly asks its sex, he assures her that it is a 'boy', but Tom settles the matter authoritatively with 'It's a bitch.' Bitch is a neutral word here, but it probably serves to suggest Tom's attitude to women, for his sense of ownership and superiority to women as mere objects relegates them to the status of 'bitches', in its pejorative sense.

The presence of the dog has a symbolic function. It is a passive figure of pathos, a victim of chance and of the whims of careless people, and it is thus a reflector of Myrtle Wilson's status and role.

In this scene of the banal, Fitzgerald handles the social comedy very effectively through the presence of the McKees. Yet even here Nick recognizes that every experience is potentially rich in meaning. A watcher down on the street might see in the high windows of the flat a romantic glow to stimulate his imagination, for the capacity to respond 'to the inexhaustible variety of life' lies within the observer.

Wilson's garage (pp. 27–8, 117–19, 130–31, 148–52)

When first taken there by Tom at the beginning of Chapter III, Nick notes the isolated position of the garage on the edge of the valley of ashes; it is a small block of yellow brick,

a sort of compact Main Street [High Street] ministering to it, and contiguous to absolutely nothing.

'Nothing' serves to identify Wilson with Gatsby in the pattern of recurrent words and images which gains significance through the novel. 'Shadow' has the same function in Nick's phrase 'a shadow of a garage'.

He assumes that such a plain exterior must conceal 'sumptuous and romantic apartments' overhead. But no act of the imagination can transfigure this scene, product of a sterile society which allows it no potential for glamour. It is a working-class ambience constructed at the bottom of the social hierarchy. The 'cement colour of the walls' is a realistic feature of 'the unprosperous and bare interior', but it also identifies the garage with dust and with death. Wilson's garage both functions as and is the ugly representation of the whole social wasteland.

When Tom, Jordan and Nick call for petrol on the way to New York in Chapter VII, Wilson is even more of a ghost figure than formerly, since he is physically sick:

> In the sunlight his face was green.

As Nick glances from Tom to Wilson, two men who have recently made the same discovery about their wives, he thinks:

> there was no difference between men, in intelligence or race, so profound as the difference between the sick or well. Wilson was so sick that he looked guilty, unforgivably guilty – as if he had just got some poor girl with child.

Nick adds a note of irony here. Wilson is spiritually as well as physically sick, but because he is a failure in the race for wealth, the only value which this society recognizes, he is made to feel guilty. Tom, on the other hand, who is indeed a seducer, is entrenched within his wealth and his caste against any such sense of guilt. The Wilsons appear to be childless – Michaelis's question to Wilson on pp. 149–50 serves to confirm this – whereas Tom, to judge from his affair with the hotel maid in Santa Barbara, might well have got 'some poor girl with child'. Symbolically, Wilson bears the brunt of society's guilt, he is the scapegoat.

When Myrtle Wilson mingles 'her thick dark blood with the dust' – the phrase has overtones of 'dust to dust' in the service for the dead – she is restored to the sterile world from which her vitality made her so eager to escape. Wrapped in blankets 'as though she suffered from a chill', she is restored to this realm of sickness. The 'hollow wailing sound' of her husband's grief – a ghost's wail – resolves itself into the words 'Oh, my God' uttered 'over and over again in a gasping moan'. Wilson's horrified moan is real, but in the final scene in the garage described by Michaelis it is put into significant relationship with Doctor T. J. Eckleburg. In the later scene, as the dust from the ash heaps mingles with the clouds forming fantastic shapes, the eyes emerge, 'pale and enormous, from the dissolving night'. Fitzgerald gives this scene of weirdly changing lights and shapes the effect of nightmare by making it the setting for Wilson's 'god'. The technique is surrealist. Fitzgerald makes the hallucinatory perception of Wilson's mind at the point of breakdown and insanity an agent for perceiving the truth about a totally materialist society.

Conclusion

The fabulous mansions of East and West Egg, together with the valley of ashes, represent alternative worlds of success and failure in a modern capitalist society. While they certainly represent on the one hand the power of wealth to create a glamour which conceals its own moral inadequacy, and on the other the ugliness of social and economic failure that no act of the imagination can transfigure, they have a symbolic function too. The two landscapes of wealth and poverty are reflections of each other, together signifying the moral identity of a society given over totally to indifference and escapism, and their relationship is accentuated by Fitzgerald's decision to bring all the main characters into disastrous convergence at the garage. But the beauty that money can achieve possesses charm and allure, and the contrasting landscapes figure as features of the characters' psychological states. For Gatsby they are irreconcilable, because he has lived so passionately with his transfiguring dream of Daisy at the expense of all other vision that once this is smashed the reality of his situation becomes intolerable. At least, this is Nick's reconstruction of his dead friend's last moments alive. For Nick too, after Gatsby's death, it is at first impossible to reconcile the glow of romantic beauty with the ugliness of a world stripped bare of beauty. Nick achieves such a synthesis when the glow of the prosaic ferry boat and his concluding recognitions about the first Dutch adventurers is placed in a shared perspective enabling him to understand that 'reality' includes imaginative vision. History/time may subsequently dismiss the transcendent dream, but it is necessary in human experience. Any reality which denies the validity of the imagination, and consequently is blind to the autonomous imagination of others, as are Tom and Daisy, is indeed a valley of ashes.

4. The Women Characters

Fitzgerald's representation of women has aroused a certain amount of adverse comment. In all his fiction women characters are decorative figures of seemingly fragile beauty, though in fact they are often vain, egotistical, even destructive and ruthless. They are very often the survivors. Prime consumers all, they are never capable of idealism or intellectual or artistic interests, nor do they experience passion. His last novel, *The Last Tycoon*, shows some development, in that for the first time the narrator is a young woman bent on trying to find the truth about the ruthless social and economic complexity of 1930s Hollywood, but she has no adult role to play in its sexual, artistic or political activities. Women characters are marginalized into the purely personal areas of experience. While working on *The Great Gatsby* Fitzgerald acknowledged that the women characters are subordinate:

... the book contains no important woman character.[1]

After the novel failed to achieve the commercial success he so much desired he wrote:

Women do not like it. They do not like to be emotionally passive.[2]

It is hard to disagree with the second statement. In conceding the important role of women readers in deciding the failure or success of a novel, Fitzgerald recognizes that the post-war woman has economic power and he implicitly connects this with her changing status.

Emancipated women

In *The Great Gatsby* Fitzgerald portrays the new social and sexual freedom enjoyed by women through the lives of Daisy, Jordan Baker and Myrtle Wilson, as well as the host of young women who attend Gatsby's parties. Tom Buchanan on the one hand advocates the old paternalism which subordinates women to the status of decorative objects of male desire, but on the other he is happy to enjoy a sensual affair with Myrtle Wilson. As readers we condemn his double standards, and Nick, as narrator, requires us to do this. But Nick's ideals of womanhood seem to differ from Tom's only in the matter of degree. He rejects Jordan Baker on the grounds of her moral inadequacy and indifference, but his descriptions suggest a concealed source of antagonism: she is 'unfeminine', androgynous, more of a boy than a 'lady'. There is a covert theme in the novel which is never openly raised by Nick as narrator or Fitzgerald as author, and that concerns the status and identity of women.

Nick makes a very strange statement at one point regarding the ethical standards of women which is certainly not the recognized truth he pretends, though it is endorsed by the actions of all the women in the novel. He is referring to Jordan Baker when he slips in this comment, deliberately making the reader an accessory to his way of thinking by the use of the pronoun 'you': 'Dishonesty in a woman is a thing you never blame deeply' (pp. 58–9). Nevertheless he does judge Jordan and throw her over. Daisy, however, is permitted to survive within this ideology – though at the price of her freedom.

A recent feminist critic has charged *The Great Gatsby* with exhibiting actual hostility towards women:

> Another American 'love story' centred on hostility to women and the concomitant strategy of the scapegoat . . . Not dead Gatsby but surviving Daisy is the object of the novel's hostility and its scapegoat.[3]

Hostility is a serious charge. While Nick's seemingly casual aside which I have just quoted expresses a patronizing contempt for women's ethical capacities, it could be explained as a manifestation of his own immaturity which Fitzgerald intended the reader to recognize. More seriously, there is not a single female character who exhibits anything but a desire for a good time and for material possessions. No woman character in the novel understands or cares about either Nick's moral preoccupations and his desire to understand experience or Gatsby's intense devotion to a dream which transcends his circumscribed self. Admittedly, this is a satirical novel and none of the other male characters pretends an interest in an inner life either, and of course Nick and Gatsby dominate this concern of the narrative. It is true to say that any interest other than a preoccupation with their own needs is beyond the women characters. In this chapter I shall argue that while the sensuous and sensual allure of women is a major feature of the novel, there is hostility towards the 'New Woman' making her appearance in post-war society. Daisy's ethereal beauty requires the connivance and protection of men to maintain it at whatever cost to her moral identity, and Tom, Gatsby and Nick are all accomplices to this.

Emancipated young women abound in *The Great Gatsby*. Nick's accounts of Gatsby's two parties focus on them, particularly as they get drunk and drift with an unspecified status through the glittering scene, gaudy with primary colours, and their hair bobbed in strange new ways, and shawls beyond the dreams of Castile. (p. 42)

They are 'wanderers', confident girls who weave here and there (p. 42), until one 'dumps down' (p. 42) a cocktail for courage before moving on to the platform to do a solo. The two girls in twin yellow dresses appear to be regulars, as one of them, Lucille, tells how she tore her dress the last time and within a week received and accepted without question a package containing a new one costing two hundred and sixty-five dollars. Later, when the dancing begins, there are 'old men pushing young girls backward in eternal graceless circles' (p. 47) and 'a great number of single girls dancing individualistically or relieving the orchestra for a moment of the burden of the banjo or the traps' (p. 48). They are an important feature of the swirling hedonistic crowds who come to Gatsby's house, swimming with the social tide, unconcerned about the sources of Gatsby's wealth. At the first party Nick notices a 'rowdy little girl' who laughs uncontrollably, and a young lady at the maudlin stage, whose tears mingle with her mascara as she sings and turn 'an inky colour', as they pursue the 'rest of their way in slow black rivulets' (p. 52) down her face. When the 'Jazz History of the World' is over,

girls were putting their heads on men's shoulders in a puppyish, convivial way, girls were swooning backwards playfully into men's arms, even into groups, knowing that someone would arrest their falls. (p. 51)

They are emancipated yet they depend upon the men. Many of them seem to belong to the world of Broadway and they contribute their share of the vulgarity which appals Daisy. Miss Baedeker has her head put under the pool by Doc Civet, much to her annoyance, because 'when she's had five or six cocktails' she always starts screaming like that. Others, who come in the following of Benny McClenahan, four at a time and all identical, are related 'to the great American capitalists' (p. 62); they are enjoying the new freedom, which can break down class barriers on such occasions as they choose, yet they too are made to constitute a harem, following the dominant male.

Wives seem to belong to the more stable world of East Egg, though the freedom and spontaneity of Gatsby's parties puts a strain on their marriages. At the first party there are the jealous wife who hisses 'like an angry diamond' (p. 52) at her husband, and the two indignant wives of 'deplorably sober men' (p. 53) who finally have to be carried 'kicking into the night'.

The accounts of Gatsby's parties are full of such vignettes presented in a tone of light irony. Fitzgerald achieves a more sombre effect at the beginning of Chapter IV, when Nick sums up the parties that summer.

On Sunday morning while church bells rang in the villages alongshore, the world and its mistress returned to Gatsby's house and twinkled hilariously on his lawn.

'He's a bootlegger,' said the young ladies, moving somewhere between his cocktails and his flowers.[4] 'One time he killed a man who had found out that he was nephew to Von Hindenburg[5] and second cousin to the devil. Reach me a rose, honey, and pour me a last drop into that there crystal glass.' (p. 60)

The men constitute 'the world', the women are merely 'its mistress'. The girls' words convey an equal lack of concern about Gatsby and the horrific recent war. The rumours about Gatsby are clearly ludicrous, but it is all a matter of indifference to them whether this is so or not. They are shown up more coldly in the morning than in the moonlight, and the reference to a rose is echoed in Nick's reconstruction of Gatsby's last moments, when he 'found what a grotesque thing a rose is' (p. 153). The girls' connection with the fragile offerings of Gatsby's garden, a rose or a crystal glass, intensifies their callousness. These are nameless young women who flit through the narrative as emancipated girls of the Jazz Age, but their new freedom merely makes blatant their complete lack of ethical concern.

Catherine, Myrtle Wilson's sister, appears to be one of them. She is 'a slender worldly girl of about thirty' (p. 32) whose pencilled eyebrows and heavy make-up characterize her as modern. She lives in a hotel with another girl and has recently returned from a trip to Monte Carlo where she lost all her money in the casino. She too has attended one of Gatsby's parties and contributes to the gossip about him. At her sister's inquest she swears that Myrtle Wilson's marriage was completely happy and 'convinced herself of it, and cried into her handkerchief, as if the suggestion was more than she could endure' (p. 155). The motive for her lies is not explained, though clearly it saved Tom from scandal; the result is that Gatsby's murder is officially pronounced to be the deranged act of an insane man. In her brief appearances Catherine is implicated in lies and gossip, and so truth appears to be a matter of no concern to her, any more than to the girls overheard on Sunday mornings.

When Daisy Buchanan begs, 'Oh, let's have fun' (p. 114), as they set off for New York in Chapter VII, she is expressing what all these young women desire: the rich society woman is no different from the rest. There might at first seem to be little in common between the débutante world in Louisville of five years previously and the lives of the girls at Gatsby's parties: however, although the former social scene maintained more decorum, it required no more awareness of public events than that shown by the girls on Gatsby's lawn. For young Daisy Fay the war was a time when nice young girls rolled bandages for the Red Cross and had a good time with the officers of nearby Camp Taylor, while the red, white and blue flags flew from their homes in patriotic display, tut-tutting disapprovingly at the flirtatious freedom now enjoyed by 'nice' girls.

Daisy and her friends had beaux to take them dancing to the 'Beale Street Blues', and the 'sadness and suggestiveness' of the music and the haunting notes of the saxophones provided a languorous rhythm while 'a hundred pairs of golden and silver slippers shuffled the shining dust' (p. 144). The language conveying Daisy Fay's wealthy 'artificial world' implies the sexual excitement which the newly fashionable blues music and their freedom to dance the night away aroused in the young women, who had nothing else to think of but affairs of the heart. This passage (when actually Nick is re-telling what Gatsby has told him on the night of Myrtle Wilson's death) provides a good example of the way Fitzgerald creates impressionistic effects by removing individuals from the central focus of the reader's interest: all those eager, aroused young women are defined by their 'golden and silver slippers', the 'shining dust' suggests their luxurious environment while at the same time implying that youth is transient. The faces are not individualized, they are 'rose petals' blown about the floor, and the effect emphasizes their transience and the fragility of feminine beauty.

At the grey tea hour there were always rooms that throbbed incessantly with this low, sweet fever, while fresh faces drifted here and there like rose petals blown by the sad horns around the floor. (p. 144)

Young Daisy Fay could not wait, she wanted her life shaped now, immediately (p. 144), and only a man and marriage could do that for a girl in her position. The young débutante of 1918–19 was separated by a social gulf from the independent girls who danced their way through Gatsby's parties in 1922, if only because she had to preserve decorum: Daisy could only be a passive object waiting for some force to shape her life, and that force materialized with the arrival in Louisville of Tom Buchanan. By contrast, the girls at Gatsby's parties have no social status to consider, they just want a good time in the frenetic scene of the early 1920s. All these girls, and the young Daisy Fay too, are portrayed as the centre of sexual interest. It is they who contribute the erotic interest in the novel, not the men. The accounts of music, dancing or gaiety which help to create the pervasive mood of luminous but evanescent beauty draw attention to their youth and allure. At the parties it is the girls who

glide on through the sea-change of faces and voices and colour under the constantly changing light. (p. 42)

The girl who does her solo act on the platform is 'in trembling opal' (p. 42), the jewel reference implying the effect of brilliant colours transformed by the lights into a soft pearl sheen. The girls may be gold-diggers, strident and comically vulgar, but Fitzgerald makes their sexual vitality the focus of these scenes.

'Gold-digger' was once a favourite metaphor for a woman who exploited her sexuality to get money out of men. While Dan Cody had once dug for gold, Ella Kaye, whose relations with the debauched millionaire were a matter for scandal in the gutter papers of 1902, found her gold mine in her lover by exerting her sexual power over him. Whether there is a connection between her arrival on Cody's yacht and his death a week later is left open to question: she certainly assumed control of his millions 'intact' after his death, and ensured that Gatsby did not deprive her of the quarter of a million dollars which Cody left him. She quite blatantly transformed 'love' into money, just as the girls at Gatsby's parties are exploiting their sexuality for a good time. More subtle aspects of the relationship between love and money are present in the case of Daisy's marriage, Gatsby's love for Daisy and even Nick's affair with Jordan.

Myrtle Wilson

She is introduced into the novel by her telephone call, which disturbs the urbane surface of Daisy's dinner party, bringing tensions between husband and wife into the open. Her social class is implied by Jordan Baker's critical remark, 'Tom's got some woman in New York' (p. 20) who hasn't 'the decency' not to disturb them at dinner (p. 20), and the force of her desire to make contact with Tom haunts the evening in the form of 'this fifth guest's shrill metallic urgency' (p. 21).

Fitzgerald has very cleverly inserted the presence of this shrill insistent intruder into the Buchanans' opulent world, which is insulated from heat, wind and everything unpleasant. Myrtle represents overt, unconcealed sexuality. When Nick meets her for the first time her vitality is in contrast with her environment, and yet she belongs to that world of indifference and death. Her flower name suggests a fleshy yet beautiful climbing plant vigorously moving upwards, but she is not allowed to realize her impossible dream.

She is older than Daisy and Jordan and the darker colours of her dresses may signify this, though more probably they are the mark of her working-class status. At her entry into the garage in Chapter II she is defined by Nick in a few lucid phrases.

... she carried her flesh sensuously ... there was an immediately perceptible vitality about her as if the nerves of her body were continually smouldering ... [she walked] through her husband as if he were a ghost ... she wet her lips, and without turning around spoke to her husband in a soft, coarse voice. (p. 28)

The implications, both here and later in Michaelis's remark about George Wilson that 'He was his wife's man and not his own' (p. 130), are that she has devoured or drained him sexually, and certainly she dominates him. Her fleshiness is voluptuous, and she emphasizes this by wearing her dress stretched tight over her broad hips.

By grammar and speech, as well as taste, Myrtle is distinguished from Tom Buchanan's exclusive world. She buys cheap scandal magazines and lets four cabs go by before selecting an impressive-looking lavender-coloured one. As they approach the block of flats on 158th Street she casts 'a regal homecoming glance about her' (p. 31), and as hostess she patronizes the subservient McKees and her sister. Her manner is again defined in sharp, clear terms that make her affectations comic. She speaks in 'a high mincing shout' (p. 33), and later

she looked at me and laughed pointlessly. Then she flounced over to the dog, kissed it with ecstasy, and swept into the kitchen, implying that a dozen chefs awaited her orders there. (p. 34)

During the course of the evening 'the room rang full of her artificial laughter' (p. 38). Yet despite her affectations and her ambition to move up in the world, she is not ludicrous. Her vitality is evident, as she dominates the people in the room. The McKees are subservient because they want to exploit her associations with Tom, and Catherine is conscious of her sister's new status in having Tom as her 'sweetie' (p. 37), but Myrtle's energy is greater than theirs. When Nick asks Catherine whether her sister doesn't like her husband, it is Myrtle who gives a 'violent and obscene' (p. 35) answer: 'Crazy about him! ... The only *crazy* I was was when I married him' (p. 37). When she comes close to Nick to talk about Tom Buchanan, 'her warm breath poured over' him (p. 38), and her language is energetic, direct and unselfconscious about her own sexual needs. Her lower-class pretensions appear comical to Nick because he judges them from a position of social superiority, but her overt sexuality impresses him. She desires Tom because of his bulky masculinity and his social style, and in a way her sexuality is a counterpart of Gatsby's romantic passion for Daisy. Myrtle Wilson desired Tom's opulence when she first saw him on the train in his dress suit and patent leather shoes.

'All I kept thinking about, over and over, was "You can't live forever; you can't live forever."' (p. 38)

No other character in the novel expresses such urgency of desire, and this is made poignant by her death. Catherine's gossip about Myrtle and Tom each living with people they can't stand and her suggestion that they ought to 'get a divorce and get married to each other right away' (p. 35) is obviously a fantasy. Myrtle Wilson can only be Tom's 'woman'. Tom makes this brutally clear when Myrtle insists on shouting Daisy's name and he puts a stop to this with 'a short deft movement' which 'broke her nose with his open hand' (p. 39).

The suddenness and violence of this shocks the reader by making Myrtle a victim of Tom's aggression. Whereas Tom merely bruises Daisy's little finger (p. 17), he breaks Myrtle's nose because she dares to storm the social barrier. There is poignancy in Myrtle's predicament at the end of the party. Nick's account omits any reference to Tom in a highly selective piece of description: the two women stumble among the crowded furniture with bloody towels; McKee stands in a drunken torpor staring at the scene; the women scold, and above their voices there is a 'long broken wail of pain' (p. 39) which is to be echoed weeks later by her husband's wailing voice. Even in her pain 'the despairing figure on the couch' is trying to protect the tapestry scenes of Versailles which give her social status. The narrative does not linger over the scene.

Myrtle does not appear again until the climax of the trip to New York in Chapter VII. When Tom, driving Gatsby's car, stops at the garage for petrol, Nick is aware of the eyes of Doctor T. J. Eckleburg keeping 'their vigil' (p. 118). Immediately after, as if to form a link with the blind eyes motif, Nick observes eyes watching Jordan Baker with 'jealous terror' (p. 119). Myrtle makes a mistake in identifying Jordan as Daisy, just as she does fatally that evening when she tries to intercept the yellow car now driven by Daisy, not Tom.

Her next appearance in the novel is in Michaelis's account at the inquest of events that day at the garage, when she is already dead. He had heard her voice, 'loud and scolding' (p. 130), in the garage and his account reinvests her with all her vitality:

'Beat me!' he heard her cry. 'Throw me down and beat me, you dirty little coward!' (p. 130)

In his attempt to assert himself by taking her West, Wilson had already told Tom,

'She's been talking about it for ten years ... And now she's going whether she wants to or not.' (p. 118)

He has 'just got wised up to something funny' (p. 118) about her trips to

New York. Michaelis's account of Myrtle's last words sustains the tone with which she is presented in Chapter III. There is venom in the way she calls her husband a 'dirty little coward', and the idea of George Wilson beating her is ridiculous: she is venting the shrill anger and desperation of a frustrated woman when her fantasy/dream is being destroyed. Curiously the mode of narration brings her to life after her death. When Tom, Jordan and Nick arrive at the garage her body is already

wrapped in a blanket, and then in another blanket, as though she suffered from a chill in the hot night. (p. 132)

Just before this,

her life violently extinguished, [she] knelt in the road and mingled her thick dark blood with the dust. (p. 131)

The moment of her death is both dramatized and given added significance by the language: there is irony in her kneeling, a posture usually associated with prayer or penitence, and so the narrative style suggests that she is paying a heavy price for her adulterous sexual life. The monosyllables and the alliteration of 'thick dark blood' and 'dust' emphasize this. The horrific details of Myrtle's injuries have implications which are also related to her sexuality: 'her left breast was swinging loose like a flap' and 'the mouth was wide open and ripped a little at the corners' (p. 131). At Nick's first meeting with her she had wet those lips voluptuously with her tongue while gazing at Tom, not even bothering to look at her husband as she ordered him out of the room to get chairs. By its reference to 'the tremendous vitality she had stored up for so long' (p. 131) and has now relinquished with such agony, the final sentence pays tribute to her sexuality, but, nonetheless, it seems that Fitzgerald makes Myrtle pay heavily for being openly sensualist. Tom certainly does not pay for his sexual transgressions.

Even when she is a cold corpse wrapped in a blanket, Fitzgerald brings dramatically to life this impulsive, coarse and rather silly woman. Dead, Myrtle Wilson is a victim of the callous rich who hold the social and economic power. By manipulation of the narrative structure he makes her death a matter of poignancy. It is also a point of crisis, one which Gatsby refuses to confront and Tom and Daisy easily brush aside: Myrtle Wilson is expendable in their scheme of things.

Buchanan tells Nick that Gatsby ran over her

'. . . Like you'd run over a dog' . . . (p. 169)
'And if you think I didn't have my share of suffering – look here, when I went to give up that flat and saw that damn box of dog biscuits sitting there on the sideboard, I sat down and cried like a baby. By God it was awful –' (p. 170)

His grief did not prevent him from slipping away with Daisy after giving Wilson Gatsby's address. Nor does it prevent him now from buying jewellery in Fifth Avenue – 'a pearl necklace – or perhaps only a pair of cuff buttons' (p. 170) – free from Nick's 'provincial squeamishness'.

Jordan Baker

Unlike Myrtle, Jordan Baker maintains a deliberate detachment which masks a determination to come out on top. Occupying a secure place in a socially influential stratum, she manipulates a patriarchal world to her own advantage. The style of writing implicates her just as much as it does Myrtle or Daisy in the tissue of images which give significance to the central ethical issues in the novel. While Myrtle, as a lower-class woman, talks without restraint, Jordan rules her life by discretion. In any case, Fitzgerald offers no access to her inner world, which is interpreted for the reader by Nick.

Jordan's name associates her with cars, the Jordan sports car and the Baker.[6] The River Jordan, traditionally associated with the life of the spirit, is, if anything, contrasted with her existence.[7] Nick's account stresses that she is a very modern emancipated woman: her slenderness, the way she holds herself, and the tan gained from her sporting life are emphasized several times. She, too, as an independent young woman, finds her way to Gatsby's parties and is prepared to wander his gardens alone, 'looking with contemptuous interest' (p. 44) down from her superior position on the marble steps. Meanwhile her escort, the persistent undergraduate who is under the mistaken impression that she is bound to yield her person to him, enjoys an 'obstetrical conversation' (p. 52) with two chorus girls. Tom's paternalistic mentality is disturbed and shocked by her independence: her family 'oughtn't to let her run around the country in this way' (p. 23). She even wears her evening dresses like sports clothes, and there is an implication that she has lost her femininity: she is androgynous.

There was a jauntiness about her movements as if she had first learned to walk upon golf courses on clean, crisp mornings. (pp. 51–2)

Jordan is characterized by her rapid, deft movements, yet there is a stillness about her on occasions. At Daisy's dinner party in Chapter I Nick first sees her posed on the huge couch in the charming drawing-room, and the descriptions draw her into Daisy's orbit of self-conscious feminine charm epitomized as flight and whiteness. She maintains her pose longer than Daisy, intimidating Nick so effectively with her composure that he almost apologizes for disturbing her.

She was extended full length at her end of the divan, completely motionless, and with her chin raised a little, as if she were balancing something on it which was quite likely to fall. (p. 14)

Nick feels threatened by her strategy of detachment, which she employs very effectively to put other people at a disadvantage. She makes him feel awkward and self-conscious.

Almost any exhibition of complete self-sufficiency draws a stunned tribute from me. (p. 14)

The choice of language implies that though he recognizes this as a very studied pose he cannot challenge it. When Jordan chooses to adopt the same pose during the scene in the Plaza Hotel, Nick is more critical because he knows she is distancing herself from any emotional entanglement in the scene.

Such 'complete self-sufficiency' creates an effective contrast in the novel with Daisy's 'bright and passionate mouth' and the inner excitement she conveys and the promises she seems to hold out. Jordan's yawns suggest a boredom and contempt which also contrasts with Daisy's radiance at the dinner table. On occasions, however, the two women seem to Nick to act in collusion. Their cool social manner and poise seem designed to make him feel socially clumsy or gauche, and he attributes these feminine ploys to their recently adopted East coast elegance.

Sometimes she and Miss Baker talked at once, unobtrusively and with a bantering inconsequence that was never quite chatter, that was as cool as their white dresses and their impersonal eyes in the absence of all desire. (p. 17)

They epitomize for Nick the sophistication of the East. As Jordan is almost twinned with Daisy as a wealthy and sophisticated East coast woman on two occasions, it would seem that this is her function in the novel. There is no place for her development in the plot.

Jordan's composure and self-sufficiency express her determined 'absence of all desire': she has her sexuality and her emotions well under control and will not give way to impulse. When Daisy follows Tom out of the room during her dinner party, obviously to expostulate with him about the telephone call, Jordan tries 'unashamedly' to catch what they are saying, for she is perfectly willing to eavesdrop and gossip to Nick about what 'everybody knew' (p. 20). Her poise and detachment are marked by Nick all the evening, yet he doubts whether even her 'hardy scepticism' allows her to forget 'this fifth guest's metallic urgency' (p. 21) when they resume dinner. She too is responsive to the sexual tension at Daisy's elegant table. When Nick and Daisy rejoin the other two in the drawing-room, Jordan maintains her appearance of complete composure as she reads to Tom a story from the *Saturday Evening Post* in a 'murmurous and uninflected' (p. 22) tone. The story, like his own, is 'to be continued'. As the glowing lamp-light engulfs her 'autumn-leaf hair' and slender arms, Nick finds her sexually attractive but morally suspect.

When he realizes that she is the golfing celebrity, he recalls having seen pictures of her 'pleasing contemptuous' (p. 23) face in magazines, but he also associates her with a piece of unpleasant gossip which he cannot recall at the time. Both attracted and repelled by her, Nick analyses her throughout their relationship, and his divided feelings create a contrast to Gatsby's total commitment to his image of Daisy. Nick is flattered to be seen in the company of a celebrity who has entry to houses otherwise socially inaccessible to himself. She yawns 'gracefully' (p. 53) in his face even as she is inviting him to call her, and he feels that 'the bored haughty face that she turned to the world concealed something' (p. 58). When he catches her out in a lie about a borrowed car he remembers details of the earlier gossip about her: she was said to have cheated in a golf tournament and then lied when the scandal seemed about to break, but the caddy and another witness had retracted their statements in time to prevent this. Nick decides that Jordan is 'incurably dishonest': because she cannot bear being at a disadvantage she will do anything, even lie or cheat, in order to maintain an advantage over others, and so maintain the power that her personality desires. He judges that she had embarked on this course when she was young, maintaining her 'cool, insolent smile' (p. 58) towards the world as a cover allowing her to satisfy 'the demands of her hard, jaunty body' without being found out. Jordan has achieved sexual freedom by means of lying or concealment. Nick also judges that she avoids relationships with clever men who might see through her, preferring instead the company of men who would never imagine a woman – that is, a lady – breaking the codes of her class.

The reader has only Nick's assessment of her character by which to judge Jordan and must always see her in an adverse light. She obviously misjudges Nick in seeing him as a safe companion who would not question her actions, because he is in fact analysing her critically all the time. Nick's very strong awareness of her lack of ethical concern puts into question the basis of his own relationships with women: he exonerates them because they have no moral nature – 'I was casually sorry, and then I forgot' (p. 59). There is always tension in the relationship with Jordan that Nick reports. He sees her as treating love as a sexual battle for advantage and ascendancy. Being in love is an uneasy state throughout the novel. Their conversation about careless driving is precisely about personal ethics in any relationship. Jordan exploits it to manoeuvre Nick into a closer relationship, thus asserting her advantage when she says, 'That's why I like you' (p. 59). She sees Nick as morally safe, a 'careful driver' who obeys 'interior rules that act as brakes on [his] desires' (p. 59), one who honours the traditional mores of gentleman and lady. The implication is that Jordan desires both the traditional protection offered to a lady and the emancipation of the modern woman. She wants the best of both worlds.

Jordan is the narrator of Daisy's affairs, never of her own. She is able to fill in details because she speaks as a woman and a former member of Daisy Fay's exclusive set in Louisville. The tone in which she recounts Daisy's drunkenness on the eve of her wedding in 1919, when the pearl necklace was cast aside in the wastepaper basket, conveys that she was rather sceptical of the strength of Daisy's resolution. She raises a doubt about Daisy's 'absolutely perfect reputation' (p. 75) since her marriage, judging that she needs 'something in her life' (p. 77) now.

As he listens to her, sitting with his arm around her in a carriage in Central Park, Nick feels attracted to 'this clean, hard, limited person, who dealt in universal scepticism' (p. 77), and is glad that, unlike Daisy, whose feminine charm is carefully preserved and protected, she has no haunting quality of mystery to turn her into 'a girl whose disembodied face floated along the dark cornices and blinding signs' (p. 78). She is a realist, not a romantic, and at this point Nick welcomes such an attitude, seeing a promise of his own emotional tranquillity in it.

At each point in the narrative Nick's response to Jordan's sexual attractiveness is countered by his critical awareness of her ethical limitations, even downright dishonesty, yet he conceals from her the strength of his disapproval. He spends considerable time with her in New York, 'trying to ingratiate himself with her senile aunt' (p. 98) and enjoying the social prestige of being her escort.

Jordan takes little part in the conversation during Daisy's luncheon party in Chapter VII. When Daisy wonders petulantly how they are to pass the time, Jordan replies prosaically that

'Life starts all over again when it gets crisp in the fall.' (p. 113)

Her seemingly trivial remark acquires significance by the end of the novel, when autumn has indeed come: with Gatsby, Myrtle and George Wilson all dead, victims of their carelessness or indifference, the rich resume their way of life in the autumn. They can avoid scandal, failure or despair and 'start all over again'.

On both social occasions at the Buchanans' house in Chapter I and Chapter VII, Jordan and Daisy are identified by their white dresses and their pose on the huge couch. When dressed for town, their 'small tight hats of metallic cloth' and 'light capes over their arms' (p. 115) suggest that smart women's fashions in 1922 provide a kind of female armour which renders them impregnable to real emotion.

During the drive to New York Jordan reprimands Tom for his snobbishness about Gatsby:

'Listen, Tom. If you're such a snob, why did you invite him to lunch?' (p. 116)

She attempts little jokes to relieve the tension when they book into the suite at the Plaza, all with Nick's tacit approval.

'It's a swell suite,' whispered Jordan respectfully, and everyone laughed. (p. 120)

When Daisy recalls her own wedding, Jordan joins them in reminiscing about the guests who attended, especially one Biloxi, and this effectively closes their ranks as members of that opulent world, while excluding Nick and Gatsby. She seems to shift in her allegiance, whereas Nick is committed to Gatsby in this tense scene. She at first tries to deflect Tom's tirade about the breakdown of family institutions leading to the breakdown of civilization and, even worse, marriage between black and white.

'We're all white here,' murmured Jordan. (p. 124)

At the urgent insistence of both Gatsby and Tom, who need supporters, she and Nick are forced to remain in the room.

Nick feels drawn closer to Jordan at the end of this scene. She adopts her neutral, noncommittal stance as Daisy wavers back towards Tom, by beginning to balance that 'invisible but absorbing object on the tip of her chin' (p. 128). When Gatsby and Daisy leave, 'isolated, like ghosts, even from our pity' (p. 129), Tom begins to triumph, but his voice is remote from them, for neither has any wish to share in his victory. On the way back, Nick remembers that this is his thirtieth birthday, a momentous occasion marking a new decade, and he takes comfort from the thought of Jordan's presence on this 'menacing' journey of life. She seems to offer him a future undisturbed by hope or despair, since 'unlike Daisy, she was too wise ever to carry well-forgotten dreams from age to age' (p. 129).[8]

But the catastrophe of Myrtle's death effaces this. When they reach the Buchanans' house Tom takes charge, advising Nick and Jordan to 'have them get you some supper – if you want any' (p. 135) in the kitchen. Nick declines to enter the house, but Jordan puts her hand on his arm:

'It's only half-past nine,' she said. (p. 135)

No explanation is given. Nick assumes that, as Tom and Daisy do, she is going to put these shattering events of the day out of her mind, and he regards the invitation as a callous act.

I'd be damned if I'd go in, I'd had enough of all of them for one day, and suddenly that included Jordan too. She must have seen something of this in my expression, for she turned abruptly away and ran up the porch steps into the house. (p. 136)

This is a crucial point in Nick's relationship with Jordan. He is joined by Gatsby as he waits for a taxi to take him home, and from this point Nick identifies with Gatsby's romantic passion rather than Jordan's opportunistic form of realism. The highly selective organization of narrative details accords him no opportunity for any intimate talk with Jordan after this, since it is designed to focus on Nick's relationship with Gatsby. As neither Jordan nor Daisy is allowed to reveal her inner feelings, the implication is that these frivolous upper-class women have none.

When Jordan telephones him in his office in New York the next day she has already avoided possible scandal by moving on to Hempstead, mentioning she is 'going down to Southampton this afternoon' (p. 147). She is her usual noncommittal self, but Nick finds her voice on this occasion 'harsh and dry', whereas usually it

came over the wire as something fresh and cool, as if a divot from the green golf-links had come sailing in at the office window. (p. 147)

Nick chooses a rather strange image: if it at least links her with grass and freshness, it strips her of conventional feminine charm with its suggestion of aggression. She has resumed her restless way of life that takes her 'between hotels and clubs and private houses' (p. 147), and makes no reference to the previous day other than to charge Nick with not being nice to her. As the eternal guest she avoids personal commitment or attachment. She is willing to adapt her plans to suit Nick, but whether he fully realizes it or not, he has resolved the problem of his own moral stance and is unable to accept her. Their desultory conversation is abruptly terminated:

I don't know which of us hung up with a sharp click, but I know I didn't care. I couldn't have talked to her across a tea-table that day if I never talked to her again. (p. 148)

Nick's revulsion is in effect a condemnation of Jordan's behaviour and indifference which the reader shares. Yet, nonetheless, Jordan's role in the novel is problematic. Nick simultaneously engages in an emotional relationship with her and a coldly critical appraisal of her dishonesty and indifference to others. He is at once disturbed by her social poise which sets the less self-assured at a disadvantage, and attracted by her sexuality. He blames her while absolving her because she is a woman. In some ways Nick is using Jordan even while she is asserting her sexual power over him. It is never an easy relationship, nor is it an appealing one.

Jordan certainly feels that Nick has been less than honest with her. When they meet for the last time Nick is on the point of returning home, dismayed and disoriented by the sophisticated East. His life there, however, includes his relationship with Jordan, in which he had undoubtedly held assumptions about the future. Her view of it is never stated.

> But I wanted to leave things in order and not just trust that obliging and indifferent sea to sweep my refuse away. (p. 168)

Nick's reference to the sea echoes his initial comment on the 'foul dust' (p. 8) that floated in the wake of Gatsby's dreams. Both 'refuse' and 'foul dust' metaphorically suggest corruption, or in Nick's case, moral dereliction, and he simply cannot leave it to time to dissolve the bonds of moral obligation that still tie him to Jordan, even if feeling is dead.

Jordan admits that her pride was hurt by Nick's rejection of her on the telephone, and it seems likely that she has armed herself with a lie.

> She was dressed to play golf, and I remember thinking she looked like a good illustration,[9] her chin raised a little jauntily, her hair the colour of an autumn leaf, her face the same brown tint as the fingerless glove on her knee. When I had finished she told me without comment that she was engaged to another man. I doubted that, though there were several she could have married at a nod of her head, but I pretended to be surprised. (p. 168)

Nick behaves, in fact, as if he believed 'any divergence from a code would be thought impossible' (p. 58), and pretends to believe her. Quite how he informed her that this was the end is not revealed; as narrator he merely reports, 'when I had finished . . .' (p. 168). When Jordan, referring to their earlier conversation, suggests that he is, after all, a careless driver, Nick replies that at thirty he is too old to keep up the pretence that a gentleman's code of honour matters to him any longer. He thus makes a clean break with Jordan, even though he is still 'angry, and half in love with her, and tremendously sorry' (p. 169).

Fitzgerald's characterization of Jordan Baker is achieved with clarity and detachment. In essence it is hostile to her as a 'new woman', who claims all the advantages of an emancipated lifestyle yet will use any strategies or duplicities to retain the traditional advantages accorded to a lady. He seems to be implying that women's status and sexual image is at a point of crisis in the post-war world. Nick does not quite know how to handle this cool, poised, independent woman of the 1920s who lays down the terms of the relationship and manipulates them to her advantage. Jordan's status in the narrative is never quite clear, other than as a foil and a contrast to Daisy.

Daisy Fay/Buchanan

Daisy Buchanan is at the very centre of the patterns of thematic imagery expressing the preoccupations of the novel.[10] The initial description of the Buchanans' luxurious estate and house finally focuses on her as its prize feature. It is she who most compels Nick's attention and interest during the evening.

In their billowing white dresses the two young women maintaining their elegant pose on the couch are associated by Nick with images of sea-birds in graceful flight (p. 13), but the language hints that they are being self-consciously alluring. Daisy exploits her femininity as well as her sexuality as she looks *up* at Nick and takes his hand in greeting. Nick's comment, 'That was a way she had', suggests that it is a feature of her practised sexual charm by which she seems to promise so much. In Chapter I Nick concentrates on the compulsive power of her voice: it is 'thrilling' (p. 14); it has a 'singing compulsion' (pp. 14–15); 'her voice compelled me' (p. 19); 'her voice glowing and singing' (p. 19); 'those breathless, thrilling words' (p. 19); 'her voice sang' (p. 20); 'her voice broke off, ceasing to compel my attention' (p. 22). Such language attributes to her the powerful enchantment of the siren on the rocks who drew passing sailors to their doom,[11] but it has other associations too.

It was the kind of voice that the ear follows up and down, as if each speech is an arrangement of notes that will never be played again. Her face was sad and lovely, with bright things in it, bright eyes and a bright passionate mouth, but there was an excitement in her voice that men who had cared for her found difficult to forget: a singing compulsion, a whispered 'Listen', a promise that she had done gay, exciting things just a while since and that there were gay, exciting things hovering in the next hour. (pp. 14–15)

Nick's extended evocation of the qualities of Daisy's voice pays tribute to her sexual allure. It does not matter that what she says is frivolous or banal, it is the musicality that fascinates by seeming to hold out promises. While on the one hand such tribute makes Daisy's sexual charm memorable and focuses her central position in the imagery relating to Gatsby's dream, on the other it rigidly imprisons her in the conventional image of woman as seductress/object of desire. As he listens to his hostess, Nick's response acts as prelude to Gatsby's cherished vision of her. Nick is thus identified with Gatsby's romanticism from the very beginning of the novel.

Yet Nick also undermines this perception of Daisy. He is able to hold a dual vision of her, just as he does of Jordan. The whole scene shifts from one view of Daisy to another:

> For a moment the last sunshine fell with romantic affection upon her glowing face; her voice compelled me forward breathlessly as I listened – then the glow faded, each light deserting her with lingering regret, like children leaving a pleasant street at dusk. (p. 19)

Daisy's radiance is dimmed by the telephone call that follows immediately after this and sets up tensions in the room.

After dinner she tells Nick of her cynicism about everything, but especially about being a woman. A few years earlier, when she learned that her baby was a girl, she had thought:

> 'I'm glad it's a girl. And I hope she'll be a fool – that's the best thing a girl can be in this world, a beautiful little fool.' (p. 22).

If this is merely a spurious note of cynicism it has little meaning, but if Daisy really meant it then it casts an interesting light on her sense of herself. When she tells Nick she *knows* everything is terrible, and all the most advanced people think so too, she sounds rather like Tom quoting his scientific books. She laughs 'with thrilling scorn' and exclaims, 'Sophisticated – God, I'm sophisticated!' (p. 22).

Released from the compelling power of her voice, Nick perceives this as yet another of the evening's poses, a gesture asserting her membership of a rather special set. He feels that she is deliberately trying to trick him into an emotional response and is therefore manipulating his feelings by the sexual power of her voice.

Daisy's voice seems to promise exciting times to come and to hint at exciting moments just past: it is just like Gatsby's dream of her, which contains no present reality, only past and future ecstasies. It appears that she chatters charmingly. Fitzgerald informs the reader too often of her charm without providing her with substance as a thinking, sentient woman. The effect is to reduce her to a charming wraith, a being who exists only as a fragile veneer, a shining radiance of Gatsby's construction, the centrepiece of Tom's wealth, rather than a woman with a personality of her own. Fitzgerald allows Daisy to exist only in the images men create of her.

During her dinner party Daisy and Jordan are often linked as members of an élite class: they move 'slenderly, languidly, their hands set lightly on their hips' (p. 16); sometimes they both talk at once, 'with a bantering inconsequence that was never quite chatter ... in the absence of all desire' (p. 17). Their boredom is a feature of their identity as wealthy, spoilt, beautiful young women: they accept the presence of the men, without bothering to put themselves out, as admiration is their due. When Jordan yawns that they ought to plan something, Daisy asks, 'What do people plan?' (p. 17). She remembers that it will soon be the longest day of the year,[12] and adds that she always watches out for it and then misses it. It is as if the tedium of life offers no variety because it is always too much trouble to enjoy an anticipated pleasure when it arrives.

Just as Myrtle obtrudes upon Daisy's dinner party with her telephone call, so Daisy is present at Myrtle's party when Catherine gossips about her and Myrtle dares to shout her name.

Jordan tells Daisy Fay's story to Nick in Chapter IV as they drive through Central Park. Naturally, she tells it from her own point of view as Daisy's younger friend who was impressed and was flattered by Daisy's notice. She observed that young Lieutenant Jay Gatsby gazed at Daisy 'in a way that every young girl wants to be looked at sometime' (p. 73), which she calls romantic. She tells Nick of the rumours that circulated soon afterwards about Daisy Fay in 1917:

... how her mother had found her packing her bag one winter night to go to New York and say good-bye to a soldier who was going overseas. She was effectually prevented, but she wasn't on speaking terms with her family for several weeks. (p. 73)

Daisy was the fairy-tale princess locked up in the tower, but 'By next autumn she was gay again, gay as ever' (p. 73). Daisy's romantic impulse was not strong enough, and the next June she married Tom.

Daisy is not allowed by the selective techniques of the narrative to tell her own story: on this occasion Jordan, so noncommittal about herself, tells it eloquently for her. Thus Daisy's emotions are filtered through another woman's knowledge, just as Gatsby's are through Nick. Only Myrtle Wilson tells her own story of her excitement as she responded to Tom's elegance and sexual power, and the way she tells it expresses her own sensuality. Fitzgerald does not attribute such overt sexuality to these upper-class women.

Daisy's second impulse to rebellion on the night before her wedding is also related by Jordan. Her pearls in the waste-basket, Daisy was clutching a letter, but her drunken speech minimized the effect of a determined effort to break away: 'Tell 'em all Daisy's change' her mine' (p. 74). It is significant that by the time Jordan and the maid got her out of the cold bath, Gatsby's letter was 'coming to pieces like snow' (p.74), and snow, like the impact of the letter, is ephemeral. As a young bride back from her honeymoon Daisy could not bear to let Tom out of her sight and would look at him with 'unfathomable delight. It was touching to see them together' (p. 75). A week later Tom's affair with the hotel maid received some publicity after the car accident. Since then husband and wife have moved in 'a fast crowd, all of them young and rich and wild' (p. 75).

Jordan's story about Daisy's life in 1917–19 shows that Gatsby exercised a hold over the older girl's feelings and memory, and even when asking about him recently after Jordan's mention of his name at her dinner party, she speaks 'in the strangest voice' (p. 76). Her languor and insincerity at her dinner party do not represent her whole personality. Yet Daisy's two past impulses to follow Gatsby which Jordan recounts were easily deflected, suggesting a consistent pattern which anticipates her behaviour on the trip to New York in Chapter VII.

It is worth reflecting on Daisy's role. Her past is recounted first by Jordan and then later by Nick as he relates what Gatsby has told him. This device of using various narrators puts all the emphasis on Gatsby's all-consuming passion and aspiration. Daisy exists as the object of his dream, a beautiful enchanted figure within a romantic dream. She is indeed 'emotionally passive'.

When Nick resumes the narration after Jordan's revelations he again emphasizes the charm of Daisy's voice. As she arrives in her open car in the rain he responds first to her 'bright ecstatic smile' (p. 82), and then to her voice.

The exhilarating ripple of her voice was a wild tonic in the rain. I had to follow the sound of it for a moment up and down, with my ear alone, before any words came through. (pp. 82–3)

Returning later to the sitting-room after tactfully absenting himself, Nick finds Gatsby glowing and radiating happiness, while it is Daisy's voice which expresses her joy: 'Her throat, full of aching, grieving beauty, told only of her unexpected joy' (p. 87). The unusual use of the word 'throat' emphasizes once again her identification with Keats's nightingale, and the implication is repeated later in this scene by the use of emotive language. When Nick leaves Gatsby and Daisy together, he judges that it is her voice

that held Gatsby most, with its fluctuating, feverish warmth, because it couldn't be over-dreamed – that voice was a deathless song. (p. 93)

The Daisy he loves is an object of Gatsby's longing *and* the creation of his imagination, and by concentrating on this feature of her charm he is able to ignore her identity as a woman of varying moods, full of inconsistencies or flaws. As a dream figure she can remain perfect. While showing her over his possessions he looks at them in a dazed way,

as though in her actual and astounding presence none of it was any longer real. (p. 88)

The intensity of his emotion puts immense pressure on Daisy. When his shirts, described in sensuous detail, become for him the symbols by which to express those five years of devotion and struggle, Daisy is shaken by feeling, and she sobs as she buries her face in them. There is nothing she can say when confronted by such devotion. In any case, the narrative allows her no depth of feeling.

So absorbed is Gatsby in his own experience at this point that he seems almost unaware of the actual Daisy beside him.

The green light burning at the end of her dock has exercised a hold over his imagination because it symbolizes the unattainable: 'It had seemed as close as a star to the moon' (p. 90). Daisy's actual presence with her arm through his reduces the green light to its ordinary identity. 'His count of enchanted objects had diminished by one' (p. 90).

What could Daisy possibly say or do to live up to such a vision of herself? There is actually little that Gatsby can say to the flesh and blood Daisy. Both need Nick's presence, and there is comic pathos when Klipspringer, the 'boarder', begins to play 'The Love Nest' on the piano at Gatsby's command. Nick speculates that already Gatsby must be experiencing a reaction, 'a faint doubt . . . as to the quality of his present happiness' (p. 92).

There must have been moments even that afternoon when Daisy tumbled short of his dreams – not through her own fault, but because of the colossal vitality of his illusion. It had gone beyond her, beyond everything. (p. 92)

It is inevitable that any discussion of Daisy turns into a discussion of Gatsby. His vision of her imprisons her in a moment in time five years earlier. Like the lovers perpetuated in clay in the eternal act of pursuit and escape in Keats's 'Ode on a Grecian Urn', Daisy is timeless in his vision.

> *She cannot fade, though thou hast not thy bliss,*
> *For ever wilt thou love, and she be fair.*[13]

In the meantime ('in between time' in Klipspringer's song) Daisy has married, had a child, experienced both passion and jealousy in her life with Tom, and possibly, as Jordan speculates, had discreet love affairs. None of this has any place in Gatsby's vision of her.

'I'm going to fix everything just the way it was before,' he said, nodding determinedly. 'She'll see.' (p. 106)

On that autumn night almost five years ago in Louisville it was the touch of *his* lips that made her 'blossom for him like a flower' (p. 107). It was *he* who breathed life into the Daisy of his vision.

After the first chapter, which functions as a prelude to the story of Gatsby's vision of Daisy, she has no autonomous life within the narrative apart from his dream. In Chapter VI, when Tom and Daisy finally drop in on one of the parties, Nick's account of Daisy is critical of her because her snobbishness destroys his own romantic vision of Gatsby's world.

... now I was looking at it again through Daisy's eyes. It is invariably saddening to look through new eyes at things upon which you have expended your own powers of adjustment. (p. 100)

Daisy's voice 'was playing murmurous tricks in her throat' (p. 101), but again Gatsby does not actually listen to what she says. Her sense of social propriety is offended by the bohemian behaviour brought by Broadway to West Egg.

She saw something awful in the very simplicity she failed to understand. (p. 103)

That is why she is fascinated by the film star, the 'human orchid of a woman' (p. 101), who maintains a totally artificial pose all the evening, allowing her director to move slowly closer to her until there is 'only a thin ray of moonlight between' (p. 103). Nick accuses her of preferring the gesture to the reality of emotion.

Gatsby's second party is the climax of the representation of Daisy as the object of his romantic vision, and it marks the end of the glowing dream. Nick notes something 'septic on the air now' (p. 102), and Gatsby is left at the end walking 'a desolate path of fruit rinds and discarded favours and crushed flowers' (p. 106). Yet there is one moment when Daisy's voice restores the magic; because she fears displacement from his vision she begins to sing as the orchestra plays 'Three o'clock in the Morning'

... in a husky rhythmic whisper, bringing out a meaning in each word it had never had before and would never have again. (p. 104)

There is a suggestion of a spell, an enchantment which transforms verbal meaning. Nick has already begun to see Gatsby's parties through 'new eyes', thus adjusting his vision to Daisy's snobbish values. Now, once she begins to sing, her voice re-establishes her magic because

> After all, in the very casualness of Gatsby's party there were romantic possibilities totally absent from her world. (p. 105)

She had, after all, responded once before in 1917 to Gatsby's proffered 'romantic possibilities totally absent from her world'.

Once again, Nick defines her feelings: she is jealous because after she has left 'some authentically radiant young girl' might bring fresh magic to Gatsby's imagination. The word 'authentically' conveys that Daisy knows she cannot live up to Gatsby's vision of her, but the reader is never given a chance to penetrate Daisy's mind, only to understand it through Nick's judgement.

Daisy is torn between her responses to Gatsby's romantic vision of herself and Tom's materialist evaluation of her, expressed by the 'string of pearls valued at three hundred and fifty thousand dollars' (p. 74) which was his wedding gift. Traditionally, the romantic imagination concerns itself with constructing a world of possibility rather than with reality, and this is what Gatsby has done. At the end of the war, young Daisy Fay was crying for the finality of 'a decision' to shape her life 'now, immediately – and the decision must be made by some force – of love, of money, of unquestionable practicality' (p. 144). Daisy Fay could not wait, romantic possibility was not enough for her. Tom Buchanan, with his enormous wealth, his aggressive sexuality and his social power, represented a reality that appealed to Daisy. Tom Buchanan 'took' her amid the full panoply of a society wedding, just as Lieutenant Jay Gatsby had 'taken' her in an illicit manner in October 1917.

> He took what he could get, ravenously and unscrupulously – eventually he took Daisy one still October night, took her because he had no real right to touch her hand. (pp. 141–2)

Daisy's own sexual needs are not mentioned in Gatsby's account any more than in Tom's perception of their relationship. She is perceived as passive, her sexuality sublimated into her voice, which is made to represent the full impact of her female personality as well as her femininity and charm. Her voice is the product of her environment, education and upbringing, as Gatsby acknowledges when he admits 'unexpectedly' just before the luncheon party at her house:

'Her voice is full of money.' (p. 115)

Gatsby's transcendent vision of Daisy, cherished over five years, has in fact defined her as a 'lady', a superior being occupying a secure place in an opulent world of material wealth. When he formed that vision in 1917 he was a poor, bedazzled outsider.

> He knew that Daisy was extraordinary, but he didn't realize just how extraordinary a 'nice' girl could be. She vanished into her rich house, into her rich, full life, leaving Gatsby – nothing. He felt married to her, that was all.
>
> . . . She had caught a cold, and it made her voice huskier and more charming than ever, and Gatsby was overwhelmingly aware of the youth and mystery that wealth imprisons and preserves, of the freshness of many clothes, and of Daisy, gleaming like silver, safe and proud above the hot struggles of the poor. (p. 142)

Only once does Gatsby, in recalling those wartime weeks of their love affair in 1917, suggest the nature of shared feeling. He remembers his last afternoon with her before being sent abroad, when the solemnity of the occasion affected them both.

> They had never been closer in their month of love, nor communicated more profoundly one with another, than when she brushed silent lips against his coat's shoulder or when he touched the end of her fingers gently, as though she were asleep. (p. 143)

This evocation of mutual tenderness is delicately handled by Fitzgerald. Gatsby was aware of Daisy as a real girl, and he behaved like any lover at the moment of parting. After her marriage, the penniless young ex-soldier without prospects – restored to the status if not the identity of James Gatz – returned to Louisville in 1919 and completed her transfiguration before he left the city. The 'charming' girl had become a symbol of his sense of personal loss and exclusion from dazzling wealth.

> He stretched out his hand desperately as if to snatch only a wisp of air, to save a fragment of the spot that she had made lovely for him. But it was all going too fast now for his blurred eyes and he knew that he had lost that part of it, the freshest and the best, forever. (pp. 145–6)

The romantic imagination invents a world of possibility, but the emotion it generates is often a sense of loss, for the transfiguring moment immediately becomes the past, the vision cannot be sustained. By placing Gatsby's recollections of the past in Chapter VIII after the catastrophe of Myrtle Wilson's death and Daisy's desertion, Fitzgerald conveys effectively how dead the past is. These memories are generated after a day of intense, sultry heat in which the real sun offers no 'benediction' (p. 145) and the brutal contingent impact of other people's desires destroys the solitary dreamer's world.

Yet when that day began, Nick could feel little sympathy with Gatsby's idealizing passion for Daisy.

That any one should care in this heat whose flushed lips he kissed, whose head made damp the pyjama pocket over his heart. (p. 110)

Daisy appears to feel the same way:

'Oh, let's have fun,' she begged him. 'It's too hot to fuss.' (p. 114)

Nonetheless, her sexual charm still manages to exert its power, even in this intolerable, stifling heat.

Her voice struggled on through the heat, beating against it, moulding its senselessness into forms. (p. 113)

It is immediately afterwards that Gatsby 'unexpectedly' acknowledges his understanding of the full implications of her sexual attractiveness by identifying it with her wealth. But he still clings desperately to the dream which has given his life meaning.

In the hotel Daisy spends some of the time in front of a mirror 'fixing her hair' (p. 120), though whether she is motivated by vanity or the desire to avoid a confrontation is never stated: the implication of Nick's narrative is the former. As Gatsby forces a showdown, she becomes desperate. He is asking the impossible of her in wanting her to deny she has ever loved Tom. She remains a passive object of the conflicting demands of the two men, as helpless to control the situation as she is later to control the big yellow car.

Her eyes fell on Jordan and me with a sort of appeal, as though she realized at last what she was doing – and as though she had never, all along, intended doing anything at all. But it was done now. It was too late. (p. 126)

Earlier in the summer, Jordan murmured that 'Daisy ought to have something in her life' (p. 77): it seems that Daisy too had wanted an affair but no more.

When she manages to say 'with perceptible reluctance' (p. 126) that she never really loved Tom, he reminds her of the occasion on their honeymoon in Kapiolani when he carried her to keep her shoes dry. The memory of the strength of Tom's protective arms and the reality of his assured social position are too powerful for Daisy, who stares 'terrified' (p. 128) between the two men as she retreats further and further into herself. She can only beg Tom to *please* stop. He magnanimously allows her to leave with Gatsby as a final assertion of his power.

The selective style of the narration passes over the horror of the car's dreadful impact on Myrtle Wilson. Gatsby tells what happened, but he is much more concerned about his relationship with Daisy and Daisy's own feelings:

Well, first Daisy turned away from the woman toward the other car, and then she lost her nerve and turned back. The second my hand reached the wheel I felt the shock – it must have killed her instantly.

'It ripped her open –'

'Don't tell me, old sport.' He winced. 'Anyhow – Daisy stepped on it. I tried to make her stop, but she couldn't, so I pulled on the emergency brake. Then she fell over into my lap and I drove on.' (p. 137)

Nick's final sneaked view through a slit in the blind strips her of all her glamour and the magic of her charm. Whereas in his first dazzled view she was a bird, a fabulous creature in white in a glass-enclosed, breeze-filled room brilliant in the afternoon sun, now the light is reduced to a slit. Even her voice is silenced: as Tom talks, 'Once in a while she looked up at him and nodded in agreement' (p. 138). Tom's male strength and his wealth close protectively around her. The cold chicken and ale – admittedly untouched – reinforce her choice of Tom's materialism rather than Gatsby's romanticism. Along with Wolfshiem's 'succulent hash' this is the only food named in the novel and it links her with his values.

When Nick telephones her after Gatsby's death her lack of feeling or moral awareness is defined by the *absence* of flowers. He calls 'instinctively and without hesitation' (p. 156), half an hour after discovering the body, but she has already gone, and she never sends 'a message or a flower' (p. 165).

Throughout most of the novel all the major motifs created by imagery of summer, flowers, moon, stars, sunshine and birdsong cohere around Gatsby's dream of Daisy, the idealized girl, but contrary images of gold, money and cars also identify her. Gatsby clings to his idealized vision of her, refusing to acknowledge to himself or Nick that she has excluded him from her world, retreated once again into 'the wealth that imprisons and preserves safe and proud above the hot struggles of the poor' (p. 142). The pattern is repeated that night as once again Daisy sits inside, Gatsby waits outside, once more excluded. Nick's view of him still relates him to moonlight, but the dream of Daisy is smashed, although he cannot admit it, and Nick knows he is 'watching over nothing' (p. 139). The actual and the dream Daisy can no longer co-exist, and Daisy vanishes from the narrative. At his final meeting with Tom, Nick recognizes 'the unutterable fact' (p. 170) that he cannot reveal Daisy's part in the accident which killed Myrtle Wilson. The code of honour of a gentleman requires that a lady's name should be protected. Daisy's role as the jewel in Tom's social crown demands that she remain passive, a woman in white, just as she was in her 'white girlhood' (p. 24), and Nick accedes to this by his silence.

Does Daisy exist more powerfully as dream than as substance for the readers? The answer, I think, is yes.[14] As the central feature of a ravishing world created by Gatsby's imaginative vision, her beauty and charm have a haunting quality: as a feature of Tom's solidly material world she is not a particularly interesting woman, and Fitzgerald fails to develop her other than as a spoilt, petulant appendage of Tom. In fact, his handling of upper-class women is limiting rather than hostile. They are presented as socially brilliant creatures who are morally and economically passive in a world which has no other role for them. Fitzgerald asserts through Nick that they are sexually exciting but he does not manage to make them sexually interesting. Perhaps he felt inhibited from creating a 'lady' who possessed sexual vitality, whereas a lower middle-class woman like Myrtle Wilson posed no such problems for him.

All three women make an effort to move outside the social conventions of their class, and all three suffer for it: Myrtle Wilson is ripped open and destroyed; Jordan Baker seems to have lost not only her integrity but her femininity too (an androgynous being, she moves like a 'young cadet' (p. 16) employing her jauntiness as a protective cover); Daisy is tempted three times to break out, but each time is easily dissuaded, and returns to her captive position, retaining it finally through the collusion of Gatsby and Nick, who do not reveal that she was driving the car that night but was unable to control the powerful vehicle. The car symbolizes freedom and mobility for women, but Jordan misuses it by dangerous driving, Daisy lets it get fatally out of control, and Myrtle is punished and destroyed by it.

The evidence of the novel suggests that Fitzgerald was fully aware of changes in women's role, and particularly in the status of the 'lady', in the post-war period, but viewed them with mixed feelings. There is an aggression in Jordan Baker, the emancipated woman, which constitutes a threat to Nick. Daisy is too much in love with her wealth and exclusive position to make a real attempt to assert her freedom, preferring the privileges of the safe, conventional passive role. Sexual love is problematic and fraught with uncertainties in this novel for both men and women.

The woman in white (p. 167)

Nick's nightmare after Gatsby's death invokes a number of images in his disturbing vision of an alienating society. They clearly relate to Gatsby's parties in their evocation of moonlight, drunken inertia and wealthy figures in evening dress.

In the foreground four solemn men in dress suits are walking along the sidewalk with a stretcher on which lies a drunken woman in a white evening dress. Her hand, which dangles over the side, sparkles cold with jewels. Gravely the men turn in at a house – the wrong house. But no one knows the woman's name, and no one cares.

The inert woman is a victim of her own desires: she is drunk. The four gentlemen are trying to maintain her in the traditional protective relationship, but she is an alien – she is nobody – possessing no position, no identity in society. Nick's nightmare reflects a disinclination to accept the diminished status of the 'lady' in the confused and confusing Jazz Age. Why else should her hand sparkle *'cold'* with jewels, rather than simply sparkle? The adjective emphasizes her lost, alienated position once she has ceased to remain content with the status of the lady, the passive, alluring object of male desire, by expressing her own sexuality.

5. Gatsby and Nick Carraway

Corrective vision

The Great Gatsby depicts a hedonistic society existing in a state of confusion and moral chaos. Those 'blue and gigantic' (p. 26) eyes of Doctor T. J. Eckleburg – 'their retinas are one yard high' – 'brood on over the solemn dumping ground' of the valley of ashes, but they see nothing. In this they are like the characters, most of whom see only what they want to see. The characters are morally blind: they fabricate 'reality', they fantasize or gossip or misread each other and themselves, they lie or betray. Gatsby's guests spread rumours about their host; Tom deceives both his mistress and his wife; Jordan Baker lies about her own actions and misjudges Nick's personality; Daisy deceives Tom, misreads Gatsby's social status from his photograph and evades the truth of Myrtle's death; Myrtle Wilson deceives her husband and mistakes Jordan Baker for Tom's wife; Wilson mistakes Gatsby for the killer of his wife; Wolfshiem mistakes Nick for a man who is 'looking for a business gonnegtion' (p. 69); the old man selling puppies on the street looks like Rockefeller. The confusions are endless. Moral blindness is a major implication affecting every one of these characters. It is a brilliant satirical stroke on Fitzgerald's part that the blank eyes on Doctor T. J. Eckleburg gazing out over the industrial wasteland are in fact a tawdry piece of sales promotion on the part of some long-dead oculist. When poor, desperate George Wilson sees in them the eyes of God there is a bitter suggestion that commerce is the new religion now.

The two central figures, Gatsby and Nick Carraway, face the problem of focusing their vision – constructing their personal images of what life means for them – within the frame of this confusing and morally disturbing land of the blind. They can give it meaning or they can reduce it to ashes. Initially Nick speaks of Gatsby as having possessed 'some heightened sensitivity to' the promises of life (p. 8), but in the autumn of 1922 he imagines Gatsby in his last moments experiencing a desolation of the spirit which reduced life to a grotesque nightmare.

pp. 153–4

If that was true he must have felt that he had lost the old warm world, paid a high price for living too long with a single dream. He must have looked up at an unfamiliar sky through frightening leaves and shivered as he found what a grotesque thing a rose is and how raw the sunlight was upon the scarcely created grass. A new world, material without being real, where poor ghosts, breathing dreams like air, drifted fortuitously about … like that ashen, fantastic figure gliding toward him through the amorphous trees.

Nick imagines Gatsby slipping from a glowing idealizing dream to a stern reality which is a nightmare. Nonetheless, the 'reality' he attributes to Gatsby is just as distorted as the dream, in the same way as his own 'reality' of the East after Gatsby's death is 'haunted … beyond my eyes' power of correction' (p. 167).

The passage just quoted is a complex one. Nick considers that Gatsby, shut off so completely from both the reality of his own corruption and recognition of 'the inexhaustible variety of life' (p. 37), has lived so long within his dream that his realization of the painful fact of Daisy's desertion must transform his view of the world completely, to the extent that even a rose must be grotesque to his eyes. The 'new world' of his life without the commanding vision of Daisy at its centre like a sun will not be real to him, even though the reality comprises the crazed figure of his murderer advancing upon him. Nick's imagined reconstruction of Gatsby's last moments brilliantly creates a surrealist picture of two figures, the hunter and the hunted (or 'the pursued, the pursuing', as Nick expressed it on p. 77), placed in a relationship of shared desolation and betrayal, both stripped of their capacity for creative, imaginative seeing, Wilson long since and Gatsby just now. Both are ghosts in a 'reality' relegating them to the wasteland and to death.

In imagining Gatsby's last moments Nick assumes that the other man was capable of seeing life in terms only of the polarities of radiant dream or ashen nightmare. Nick himself feels threatened by the wasteland after the betrayals and deaths he has witnessed. Throughout the novel he has been carried along by the force of other characters' desires, invited to look at life through their eyes, to see their 'reality' as they want him to see it and to share the worlds they have created for themselves, but he has managed to distance himself sufficiently to judge them critically. Now he is alone. It was always Gatsby's world that intrigued him most by its seductive beauty, and though critically alert to its insubstantiality and ambivalence, he was drawn to the man who created it on such a grand scale. After Gatsby's dream world has been smashed, Nick identifies more closely with him because he sympathizes with the impulses that led him to construct it. *His* is the only version of Gatsby's inner world in the moments before his death that the narrative offers. Although he is composing a very graphic picture of Gatsby's mental landscape and superimposing on it the advancing figure of Wilson, he is also identifying with another character's desolation, and in fact it is he, as narrator, who is defining it. In a way Nick and Gatsby are dual versions of the same experience, and Nick's experiences in the East reflect the moral temptations already experienced by the older man, though emancipated Jordan is no dream girl like Daisy. Gatsby is the real 'guide . . . pathfinder . . . original settler' (p. 9) in the confusing contemporary landscape of fabulous wealth that Nick prides himself on being as he settles in West Egg.

After Gatsby's death Nick comes to realize that polarities of the ecstatic vision and the nightmare view of life are equally distorting ways of seeing reality. As 'pioneers', adventurers and 'settlers' in the contemporary world, which has discarded the traditional ethics and beliefs afforded by religion and replaced them with the prevailing power of a materialism producing fabulous wealth at one extreme and ailing ghost-figures at the other, it is not easy for Gatsby or Nick to achieve a corrective vision. Gatsby dies in trying to maintain his dream of Daisy, and it is left to Nick to make the attempt.

Both young men are drawn by the allure and style of this world: as a seventeen-year-old Gatsby saw in it all the 'beauty and glamour' imaginable, and after the war he gravitates to New York, the centre of wealth. In 1922 Nick too decides to try his fortune in that city; once there, he might so easily have succumbed to the ethics of the world Tom, Daisy and Jordan inhabit or have accepted the lucrative 'side line' (p. 80) offered by Gatsby in payment of a favour received, just as Gatsby had succumbed to first Cody's and then Wolfshiem's world. Nick too might have become a careless driver, aware only of his own desires, blind to the existence or needs of others.

Gatsby has yielded to the power of illicit wealth. He knows exactly how his transactions stand in relation to the law, and has, for example, taken care to stand in good stead with the commissioner of police by means of a 'favour' (p. 67) which gives him exemption from traffic laws, if nothing more. Fully aware that Wolfshiem ought to be in jail for playing lucratively with 'the faith of fifty million people' (p. 71), he merely comments:

'They can't get him, old sport. He's a smart man.'

Yet he has refused to acknowledge the presence of the wasteland within his all-consuming dream of a world graced by Daisy's presence at its centre. When Nick finally leaves him standing on the steps of his grandiose mansion in the familiar pose of a host speeding the departing guest, he is reminded of the first party he attended there.

The lawn and drive had been crowded with faces of those who guessed at his corruption – and he had stood on those steps, concealing his incorruptible dream, as he waved them goodbye. (p. 147)

Nick's rather graceful paradox – the deliberate juxtaposing of 'corruption' and 'incorruptible' – pithily expresses the paradox of Gatsby's personality by discriminating between the man's inner world and the life in which he is implicated. The paradox had existed from the moment young James Gatz adopted a new identity to suit his entry into the world of the debauched millionaire Dan Cody. The luxurious yacht represented the beauty he craved, and that was enough for him despite the aura of 'the savage violence of the frontier brothel and saloon' (p. 97) surrounding its owner. Young James Gatz's dreams had seemed to offer a promise 'that the rock of the world was founded securely on a fairy's wing' (p. 96), and his own overnight transformation from adolescent hobo to elegantly clad young man aboard a millionaire's yacht appeared to confirm it. During the war Daisy and her luxurious lifestyle both extended his conception of the protective power of wealth and provided him with an emotional focus for his need to endow that world with beauty and grace.

Late in their brief relationship Nick learns from Gatsby the story of his love affair with Daisy Fay in 1917. He dismisses it as 'appalling sentimentality' (p. 107), yet he is reminded of something he has heard 'a long time ago'. The final phrase might refer to his childhood but it might equally suggest a mythical past of human innocence. It is

an almost elusive rhythm, a fragment of lost words,

but Nick cannot recall them:

and what I had almost remembered was incommunicable for ever.

The nature of those elusive fragments is not revealed because it is 'incommunicable' and it is left to the reader to try to find them, the implication being that they are a part of some lost vision of innocence, an image of a self not yet corrupted or divided by desire. Nick recognizes in Gatsby's dream a quest for this, and as narrator he seeks to draw the reader into his awareness that this is a universal experience.

Gatsby sought to overcome the corrupting processes of time and his adult experience by creating his own radiant inner vision of innocence which would be realized through Daisy. In this way he superimposed an invented gloss upon the wealth which gave him access to the beauty he craved. Failing to perceive the immaturity behind this desire, he remained locked in a time warp of his imagination. It is left to Nick to find the corrective vision which will allow him to achieve an integrated identity in the reality of a morally chaotic world of modern wealth and technological power by leaving a space for the creative imagination without which the world would be a valley of ashes. Whether he really achieves this is open to question. I will examine the two characters separately in this chapter before returning to this question.

Gatsby is presented almost entirely through Nick's puzzled and often disapproving eyes. In confronting this mysterious but always morally ambivalent figure, Nick is made to face awkward aspects of his own personality and some ethical dilemmas of his own.

Jimmy Gatz/James Gatz/Jay Gatsby/'Mr Nobody from Nowhere'

An isolated figure

Throughout the novel Nick provides some powerful visual impressions of Gatsby, adding up to a pattern of perspectives of him which emphasize his solitude and isolation. Again and again, Nick gazes at him as he stands in a rather stiff, formal pose, with an arm outstretched or raised against a background of light and shade, usually at night. These gestures are expressive of a romantic craving or of a farewell before he retreats into the world of his self-created dream, which only he can preserve intact and inviolate. As the gestures are strongly characteristic I will list them here.

p. 25 Nick's impulse towards friendly contact with his neighbour is frustrated by the intentness of Gatsby's gaze:

Involuntarily I glanced seaward – and distinguished nothing except a single green light, minute and far away, that might have been the end of a dock.

p. 51 At Gatsby's first party the girls swoon back into the men's encircling arms.

But no one swooned backward on Gatsby, and no French bob touched Gatsby's shoulder, and no singing quartets were formed with Gatsby's head for one link.

p. 56 As the guests leave, the emptiness of the house seems to cut him off from ordinary experience.

A sudden emptiness seemed to flow now from the windows and the great doors, endowing with complete isolation the figure of the host, who stood on the porch, his hand up in a formal gesture of farewell.

pp. 138–9 Nick does not tell Gatsby that he has seen Daisy and Tom sitting in the kitchen with the 'plate of cold fried chicken between them, and two bottles of ale' and Gatsby is determined to wait in case Daisy should signal.

He put his hands in his coat pockets and turned back eagerly to his scrutiny of the house, as though my presence marred the sacredness of the vigil. So I walked away and left him standing there in the moonlight – watching over nothing.

p. 145 Nick's narration of Gatsby's own account of his last despairing journey to Louisville in 1919 after Daisy's marriage to Tom has taken her from the city portrays him as a lonely, questing figure.

He stayed there a week, walking the streets where their footsteps had clicked together through the November night and revisiting the out-of-the-way places to which they had driven in her white car.

p. 147 Nick's last glimpse of Gatsby alive sustains the picture of his isolation.

His gorgeous pink rag of a suit made a bright spot of colour against the white steps, and I thought of the night when I first came to his ancestral home, three months before.

p. 154 Nick's intense awareness of Gatsby's isolation in death begins to operate when he and the servants hurry down to the swimming pool. The account avoids all mention of the body.

p. 156 Gatsby's solitude in death features as an implicit condemnation of society.

Then, as he lay in his house and didn't move or breathe or speak, hour upon hour, it grew upon me that I was responsible, because no one else was interested – interested, I mean, with that intense personal interest to which everyone has some vague right at the end.

A society bent only on the immediate satisfaction of desires strips both life and death of any significance. The valley of ashes is the major symbol of this careless materialist society. Paradoxically, Gatsby has contributed to that sterile wasteland by his own rise to wealth

A mysterious and ambivalent figure

Gatsby is presented entirely through the medium of Nick's oscillating responses to him, and it is through friendship with such a morally ambivalent man that Nick comes to face aspects of his own ethical nature, thereby experiencing a crisis of identity which offers him alternative visions of hope or despair. Despite Nick's repeated critical appraisals of him, there is something exotic about Gatsby which appeals to his imagination, and it is finally through Nick's imaginative response that Gatsby is ultimately judged.

Before he meets Gatsby the gossip and rumour rife among all those who have enjoyed his bounty turns him into a mysterious and alien figure: Catherine tells Nick that 'they say' Gatsby is a nephew of Kaiser Wilhelm (Imperial Head of the German State until the end of the First World War), and she is 'scared of him' (p. 35); at the party Nick's companions whisper what 'Somebody told me' – Gatsby has killed a man, or been a German spy or been in the American army, and one adds, 'I'll bet he killed a man' (p. 45). All this serves to stimulate Nick's curiosity. In the course of the party Jordan tells Nick that Gatsby claims to be 'an Oxford man', but she does not believe him and she refuses to speculate:

'He's just a man named Gatsby.' (p. 50)

But Nick needs to give shape to a background for Gatsby since

young men didn't – at least in my provincial inexperience I believed they didn't – drift coolly out of nowhere and buy a palace on Long Island Sound. (p. 50)

Yet this precisely is what Gatsby has done. Fitzgerald deliberately gives him almost mythic status by not specifying Gatsby's business affairs in detail. Gatsby's own stories of inherited money (pp. 64 and 87) lost in the panic of war are transparent fabrications: his vague explanation of the three years it took him to earn the money to buy his house in 'the drug business' and then 'the oil business' (p. 87) probably bears some relation to the truth, but it is certainly not the whole truth.

Gatsby contributes to the mystery that surrounds him by telling Nick a spurious 'history' on the way to New York in Chapter IV. Nick notes that he hurries over the phrase about being at Oxford, using such terrible clichés that listening to him is like 'skimming through a dozen magazines' (p. 65). Yet, basically, he appears to be telling the truth about the war: he has a distinguished and heroic war record.

In the Argonne Forest[1] I took the remains of my machine-gun battalion so far forward that there was a half mile gap on either side of us where the infantry couldn't advance. We stayed there two days and two nights, a hundred and thirty men with sixteen Lewis guns, and when the infantry came up at last they found the insignia of three German divisions among the piles of dead. (pp. 64–5)

When Gatsby produces the photograph with the spires of Oxford in the background together with his medal, the Order of Danilo,[2] 'For Valour Extraordinary' from 'little Montenegro down on the Adriatic Sea' (p. 65) (now part of Yugoslavia), Nick's doubts disappear.

> Then it was all true. I saw the skins of tigers flaming in his palace on the Grand Canal; I saw him opening a chest of rubies to ease, with their crimson-lighted depths, the gnawings of his broken heart. (pp. 65–6)

Nick's relief is ludicrously exaggerated, and the language of this passage admits as much, for the 'flaming' tiger skins and the 'chest of rubies' are the stuff of fairy tales or films.[3] Nick knows that Gatsby's story of his childhood is a rather unoriginal fantasy, but he *wants* to believe in him. As they drive over the Queensboro Bridge, casting light from all the glass and nickel of Gatsby's magnificent car, Nick thinks:

'Anything can happen now' . . . Even Gatsby could happen. (p. 67)

Nick's attitude towards Gatsby is thus ambiguous. At first – perhaps all the time – he is morally critical of him, and in fact says 'I disapproved of him from beginning to end' (pp. 146–7), but he is always drawn towards him. He sees Gatsby in a double perspective: one view puts him into a romantic and heroic glow, while the other rejects him as 'simply the proprietor of an elaborate road-house next door' (p. 63). It is just such a double perception that Nick is required to practise at Gatsby's first party when the stranger talking to him turns out to be his host. The passage defines Gatsby's ambivalence for Nick.

p. 49

He smiled understandingly – much more than understandingly. It was one of those rare smiles with a quality of eternal reassurance in it, that you may come across four or five times in life. It faced – or seemed to face – the whole eternal world for an instant, and then concentrated on *you* with an irresistible prejudice in your favour. It understood you just so far as you wanted to be understood, believed in you as you would like to believe in yourself, and assured you that it had precisely the impression of you that, at your best, you hoped to convey. Precisely at that point it vanished – and I was looking at an elegant young rough-neck, a year or two over thirty, whose elaborate formality of speech just missed being absurd. Some time before he introduced himself I'd got a strong impression that he was picking his words with care.

Nick depicts two Gatsbys in the following terms: one a figure of rare charm who offers you a romantic view of yourself so long as you accept his romantic image of himself; the other an uncultured young man who adopts a stiffly formal manner in order to conceal his social deficiencies. Nick's first impression relates to Jay Gatsby, while the after-image refers to James Gatz, although Nick has no knowledge of him. One is a romantic self-construct, the other the product of his upbringing as a poor boy in the Midwest. The language and rhythms of the passage intimate just how fragile and vulnerable this adopted identity is and how dependent on the observer's entering into a complicity in make-believe, bribed or charmed by the promise of reciprocal wish-fulfilment. Nick's intuition provides a valuable key to Gatsby's identity and his vulnerability.

What the carefully contrived ordering of the novel gradually reveals through the medium of Nick's perceptions is the precariousness of the fiction of Jay Gatsby's romantic identity. Gatsby has invented a self, but he is a split personality: he needs to synthesize the two selves by reclaiming that lost moment in time when he kissed Daisy Fay in 1917, thereby glimpsing a unified self that would fulfil his aspirations through love. Until he can achieve that he remains indeed 'Mr Nobody from Nowhere'.

Faithful lover and wealthy parvenu

Gatsby affects a certain style of dress which ostentatiously proclaims his wealth. As young James Gatz he had worn 'a torn jersey and a pair of canvas pants' (pp. 94–5) which at night he would throw in a tangled heap on the floor. Dan Cody effected the transformation to Jay Gatsby by fitting him out in smart yachting clothes. Now he has a man in England to buy his clothes, and as evidence of his wealth he casts his 'rich soft heap' (p. 89) of shirts higher and higher for Daisy's benefit and inspection as he shows her over his house. He wears a 'caramel-coloured suit' (p. 63) or a 'white flannel suit, silver shirt and gold-coloured tie' (p. 81), deliberately adopting styles to flout the conventions of a gentleman's dress. Sartorially 'correct' Tom Buchanan despises him for wearing 'a pink suit' (p. 116). While in Tom's view his clothes may seem outrageous, towards the end of the novel they are given other associations. For instance, on Gatsby's last night alive as he waits outside Daisy's window for the signal that will never come, Nick notes 'the luminosity of his pink suit under the moon' (p. 136), and when bidding his last goodbye to Gatsby the next morning he notices how 'his gorgeous pink rag of a suit made a bright spot of colour against the white steps' (p. 147). By association with moonlight and whiteness the suit is no longer a mark of extravagance – or even bad taste – but is made an attribute of the man who created a transcendent dream, and by this token is turned into a mark of innocence and faith. The pervasive imagery permits such fluid changes of significance.

Gatsby's huge and ostentatious yellow car holds a central place in the narrative and it is equally ambivalent. Gatsby is surely being modest in calling it 'pretty' as Nick gazes at it.

p. 63

I'd seen it. Everybody had seen it. It was a rich cream colour, bright with nickel, swollen here and there in its monstrous length with triumphant hat-boxes and supper-boxes and tool-boxes, and terraced with a labyrinth of wind-shields that mirrored a dozen suns. Sitting down behind many layers of glass in a sort of green leather conservatory, we started to town.

While Nick's tone and language are ironic, words such as 'swollen' and 'monstrous' acquire sinister associations: the person inside this garish greenhouse is cut off from reality. Tom refers contemptuously to its vulgarity in calling it 'this circus wagon' (p. 115), just as he terms Gatsby's house a menagerie, but he insists on driving it because the sheer power it represents impresses him. When Nick first rides in it to New York he gives it an association with light –

With fenders spread like wings we scattered light through half Astoria . . . (p. 66)

– and the huge car with all its nickel and glass takes on almost mythical associations along with its exotic owner. Yet immediately after this, when stopped for speeding, Gatsby reveals the corrupting power of wealth by producing his card with the Police Commissioner's signature on it. It is this monstrous machine which rips Myrtle Wilson's breast from her body and becomes the 'death car' (p. 131).

Like most of his possessions, the figure of Gatsby is contradictory. He created a new self when he seized the 'destiny' offered by Dan Cody and his yacht, so that Jimmy Gatz, whose name perhaps signified a poor immigrant of central European stock at the beginning of the century, became romantically named Jay Gatsby. Yet Fitzgerald must have created the name with ironic intentions: a 'gat'[4] is a slang term for a pistol, and so Gatsby's name is a particularly effective pun at a time of gangland activity during the prohibition era.

While writing the novel Fitzgerald was criticized for the vagueness of the characterization of Gatsby, and in his letters he admits that the character changed in the process of writing. At one point he writes: 'I've brought Gatsby to life. I've accounted for his money.'[5] Yet this vagueness contributes to our impression of Gatsby as a mythic as well as a self-invented figure. When Fitzgerald brings the novel to a climax in Chapter VII he creates a dramatic scene dependent on dialogue for its effects, and it is here that Gatsby's business activities are brutally disclosed by Tom.

'She's not leaving me!' Tom's words suddenly leaned down over Gatsby.

'Certainly not for a common swindler who'd have to steal the ring he put on her finger.' (p. 127)

Tom's 'investigations' have revealed that Gatsby and Wolfshiem bought up side-street drugstores in New York and Chicago and sold grain alcohol over the counter.[6] Tom's friend Walter Chase has served a jail sentence for his part in their affairs, and he could have them up on the betting laws if he weren't too frightened to speak: now they are on to something much bigger which Walter daren't even mention. After Gatsby's death, the telephone calls continue and a man called Slagle, thinking he is talking to Gatsby, tells Nick young Parke has been picked up 'when he handed the bonds over the counter' (p. 158). Presumably these are stolen bonds whose numbers have been recorded. Fitzgerald thus uses the dramatic structure of the novel to make the disclosures of how Gatsby's activities operate during the tense moment when Daisy is forced to choose between the two men and later, after his death.

Gatsby's fabulous wealth is a product of the social and moral disorder of the time, and he is fully implicated in these: yet the sources of his wealth, in his view, bear no relation to his inner need to find his ideal self that would bring order and beauty into his life. His wealth has significance for him only in relation to Daisy, because only through his love for her can he realize his ideal self. One detail of the tour of his house in Daisy's presence exemplifies this. All the rooms through which they progress are referred to in the plural to give an impression of their spuriousness and futility, as well as their ostentation:

... Marie Antoinette music-rooms and Restoration Salons ... dressing-rooms and poolrooms, and bath-rooms with sunken baths. (p. 88)

When they arrive at his own suite of rooms Daisy enjoys touching the brush of a 'toilet set of dull gold'. But for Gatsby the reality of his wealth is already becoming unreal now that the Daisy of his dream has materialized in the shape of the real woman. The nature of reality is a central issue in the novel affecting all the characters whether they realize it or not. The 'real' Gatsby is both rough-neck and romantic lover, and the real Daisy is the girl whom he loved in 1917 as well as Tom's wife and the mother of a child. Gatsby clings to the images of himself as romantic, faithful lover and Daisy as radiant girl, since they constitute the personae of his dreams. If Fitzgerald had allowed Gatsby to speak for himself or had introduced intimate scenes relating to Gatsby and Daisy's love affair he might have lost that balance between inner and outer worlds, subjective perception and 'reality', which is held in tension throughout the novel. The structure and style, together with the use of Nick as narrator of Gatsby's story, who undergoes his own crisis of identity, all contribute to this balance and the final synthesis of the two.

Gatsby's past is inserted at various points into the events during the summer of 1922, the story of his creation of a transfigured and transfiguring Daisy being completed only on the night before his death.

Nick fills out his impressions of Gatsby, piecing together scraps of information in order to understand the other man's life, and by doing so he manages finally to construct a coherent image of life in a chaotic and impersonal world which impedes all efforts to establish a personal ethic other than callous indifference or greed. It is only a glimpsed vision of synthesis which Nick attains at the end of the novel. He still has to put it into practice, and his telling of Gatsby's story is the first step towards this. He perceives Gatsby's transfiguring love as both a ludicrous and a heroic act of defiance of such a world, and in his final vigil on the Long Island shore he acknowledges the impossibility of the dream and the validity of the impulse.

Only after Gatsby's death is Nick in full command of the outline of his life.

Gatsby's past

Chapter IV, pp. 63–6 Gatsby tells Nick 'God's truth' about his childhood. Nick dismisses the fictions but thinks that the war record and the period at Oxford must be true. This follows the first party.

Chapter IV, pp. 72–6 Jordan gives an account of Daisy's life from October 1917 when she was having an affair with Lieutenant Jay Gatsby up to 1919 when she married Tom. This follows Nick's lunch in New York with Gatsby and Wolfshiem.

Chapter VI, pp. 94–7 Nick gives an account of Gatsby's self-transformation at seventeen when he met Dan Cody. This follows Daisy's reunion with Gatsby, though Nick points out that he learned it later – actually on Gatsby's last night alive, 'a time of confusion when I had reached the point of believing everything and nothing about him' (p. 108).

Chapter VI, pp. 106–7 Nick relates Gatsby's moment of transcendent feeling in kissing Daisy Fay back in the autumn of 1917. This follows Gatsby's second party.

Chapter VIII, pp. 141–5 Nick gives a further account of Gatsby's relationship with Daisy in the autumn of 1917, when she became a 'grail' to be worshipped in her opulent surroundings, from which his poverty excluded him. He fills in further details of Gatsby's war record, and his despair when he visited Louisville, now bereft of Daisy, in 1919. This follows Myrtle Wilson's death and Nick's sense of the betrayal of Gatsby by Daisy, and it is part of the same long conversation reported in Chapter VI.

Chapter IX, pp. 158–60, 163–5, 179–81 Mr Henry Gatz, Gatsby's father, says that his son was bound to succeed, and to prove it shows Nick a tattered copy of young Jimmy Gatz's boyish schedule and General Resolves for getting on. The fact that Gatsby lies dead, betrayed and abandoned, gives this a certain irony.

Chapter IX, pp. 162–3 Meyer Wolfshiem reminisces about his first meeting with Gatsby, 'a young major just out of the army', and how he put him on the road to success. Again, this success is given ironic implications by Wolfshiem's care not to associate himself now with his dead partner.

Although this information is presented in a seemingly random or contingent way, the effect is to build up a coherent picture of the intensity of Gatsby's dream by means of climactic moments of his emotion, while at the same time making it subject to Nick's ironic scrutiny and comment. Gatsby's death is given added poignancy by the subsequent naiveté of Mr Gatz's pride in his son's success. Nick's feelings towards Gatsby are constantly changed and modified as a result of such different perspectives.

Gatsby and time

Jordan Baker gives Nick the first clue to the relationship between Gatsby and his past when she tells him,

'Gatsby bought that house so that Daisy would be just across the bay.' (p. 76)

Nick then understands something that had previously puzzled him about his neighbour's rapt pose and obvious desire for solitude on the first night he glimpsed him.

Then it had not been merely the stars to which he had aspired on that June night. He came alive to me, delivered suddenly from the womb of his purposeless splendour. (p. 76)

The imagery of birth is used significantly again of Gatsby just after this by Nick's insertion into the narrative of what Gatsby was later to tell him on his last night alive.

p. 95

The truth was that Jay Gatsby of West Egg, Long Island, sprang from his Platonic conception of himself. He was a son of God – a phrase which, if it means anything, means just that – and he must be about His Father's business, the service of a vast, vulgar and meretricious beauty. So he invented just the sort of Jay Gatsby that a seventeen-year-old boy would be likely to invent, and to this conception he was faithful to the end.

The Greek philosopher Plato suggested that the material world we ex-perience is a mere shadow of the ideal world which constitutes reality. Therefore the identity of Jay Gatsby as an ideal conception of himself is cherished by young James Gatz as he beats his penniless way along the shore of Lake Superior. On meeting Dan Cody he presents a ready-made identity produced by the fantasies with which his imagination has fed his craving for a different kind of life. Significantly, Nick links young James Gatz's dreamworld with moonlight, contrasting them both in turn with the harsh reality of time, as he does on other occasions too. The language of the passage is highly associative, 'a son of God' and 'His Father's business' evoking the perfection of Christ and his act of total dedication. However, in the phrase that follows it –

a vast, vulgar and meretricious beauty (p. 95)

– irony is introduced to re-emphasize that Gatsby is dedicating himself to a beauty that only wealth can create or buy and that is, in fact, morally suspect.

This beauty takes material form when young James Gatz sees in Dan Cody's yacht 'all the beauty and glamour in the world' (p. 96). Before the yacht turned up as his 'destiny' he had only the fantasies created through his 'overwhelming self-absorption'. Cody provides him with the first focus for his fantasies: Daisy will provide him with the second by allowing him to invest it with love.

For a while those reveries provided an outlet for his imagination; they were a satisfactory hint of the unreality of reality, a promise that the rock of the world was founded securely on a fairy's wing. (pp. 95–6)

Again, there is irony in Nick's juxtaposition of the phrases 'rock of the world' and 'fairy's wing'. Young James Gatz elevates his wish-fulfilment to a status well above the reality of his poverty. That is why he seizes the chance of a relationship with Dan Cody as signifying his destiny. By the end of his five years on Cody's yacht,

the vague contour of Jay Gatsby had filled out to the substantiality of a man. (p. 97)

But the contour consisted only of an immature seventeen-year-old's romantic self-idealization. Gatsby is therefore trapped in a timeless past which allows him no chance to develop any understanding of life's complexity. Rational thought or self-questioning would quickly destroy it. Nick further discovers that Gatsby's ideal of himself is rooted in his idealization of Daisy in 1917. At the moment on the sidewalk 'white with moonlight' (p. 106) when he kissed Daisy and 'forever wed his unutterable visions to her perishable breath' (p. 107), he felt his dream to be realized. Henceforward he was to be obsessed by the need to re-live that moment.

The language in this passage suggests multiple layers of meaning: Daisy's 'perishable' breath acts as a reminder that she is human, subject to the change and decay of time; but 'incarnation' conveys the intensity and dedication of Gatsby's perception of the spiritualized moment. The ladder which mounts to 'a secret place above the trees' marks the extent to which he is cutting himself off from ordinary experience in his aspiration to achieve a higher subjective ideal of himself. The imagery also suggests how difficult it is to articulate or even give shape to such vague longings:

... he could climb to it, if he climbed alone, and once there he could suck on the pap of life, gulp down the incomparable milk of wonder. (pp. 106–7)

Nick condemns Gatsby's 'appalling sentimentality' which, however, appeals to his own sense of a vague, indefinable longing for an ideal self. While Nick is content to admit the existence of such a desire, Gatsby has centred his life upon it. For him to achieve it, Daisy must obliterate three years of her adult married life and say to Tom, 'I never loved you' (p. 105). He is too self-absorbed to see that he is asking the impossible.

'Can't repeat the past?' he cried incredulously. 'Why of course you can!' (p. 106)

Undoubtedly, the language conveying the kiss is inflated. But it is the significance which Gatsby attributes to the kiss that is being conveyed. It is the great turning point in his life, the moment of revelation.

His all-consuming vision is totally egocentric. Daisy is the object of his worship, but she is allowed no warm humanity, no autonomous life of her own as a woman. As Nick realizes at the tea-party in Chapter V, the symbolic green light has more meaning for him than Daisy with her frivolity and chatter. He does not listen to what she says, and it is likely that he did not in 1917, when 'she used to be able to understand' (p. 106).

Before this experience Gatsby had been emotionally indifferent to women. A sexually attractive young man, he was pursued rather than pursuing and was content with casual affairs. In his initial acquaintance with Daisy he was happy to treat her in the same way as he had those other women.

> So he made the most of his time. He took what he could get, ravenously and unscrupulously – eventually he took Daisy one still October night, took her because he had no real right to touch her hand. (pp. 141–2)

The language in this passage is interesting. There is irony in the phrase 'he made the most of his time': time for him *then* was the present, as it is for Wolfshiem who 'just saw the opportunity of making money' (p. 71) by an act of corruption, or for Tom or Daisy, reality for them being the satisfaction of desire *now*. The words 'ravenously and unscrupulously' implicate Gatsby in their world, through a suggestion of the carnivorous beast of prey. Daisy was at first simply a 'desirable' (p. 141) object shut away inside the 'indiscernible barbed wire' of social caste which excluded him from the company of 'nice' girls.[7] Once he has taken her – the word is a cliché in this context, but it suggests plunder – he discovers he has 'committed himself to the following of a grail' (p. 142). A casual sexual relationship has been transformed into romantic love, and Gatsby finds himself fixed in that moment of time past, and looking forward ecstatically to some transfiguring moment in the future.[8] The language used employs traditional associations of the spiritual quest. The grail was the cup in which Joseph of Arimathea was said to have caught the blood of Christ on the Cross: it became the sacred object of quest by knights in Arthurian legend which only the pure were allowed to undertake. Apart from this one word, which portrays Gatsby as a votarist engaged in a sacred pursuit of an object symbolizing the attainment of ideal human nature, the language on pp. 141–2 is concerned with the material goods with which Daisy is surrounded. Gatsby's deepest experience is presented in a dual perspective: the mystery which she represents for him emanates from her 'beautiful house', 'this year's shining motor-cars', 'her rich house'; even her porch shines with the 'bought luxury of star-shine'. Daisy is a gem in a rich setting, 'gleaming like silver, safe and proud above the hot struggles of the poor' (p. 142). Her attractiveness and sexual desirability are inseparable from her wealthy environment in the mind of the penniless young man who had 'no comfortable family standing behind him' (p. 142).

Even as Gatsby attains his desire in reunion with Daisy, Nick's account contributes an ironic reference to time. Commanded to play, Klipspringer accompanies their silent ecstasy with a popular song of the day:

> *'One thing's sure and nothing's surer*
> *The rich get richer and the poor get – children.*
> *In the meantime,*
> *In between time –'* (p. 92)

Gatsby is fully involved in the meantime of history in getting richer by illegal means which exploit history. Even so, he believes he can step aside into a timeless moment of personal vision.

The nature of Gatsby's dream

There is irony in the fact that Dan Cody's yacht should represent a first glowing vision of 'all the beauty and glamour of the world' (p. 96) for young James Gatz. Nick's narration of this episode clearly places the sources of Cody's fortune in a savage and bitter struggle for wealth, which was sustained during the millionaire's life by the 'infinite number of women who tried to separate him from his money' (p. 96). Wealth and sex are closely related in this vicious and greedy world of plunder, which renders life meaningless by denying any altruism in human endeavour: life becomes a species of jungle in which the immediate satisfaction of desire is the only value. However, drawn irresistibly by the magnet of wealth, and having taken Daisy in an act of sexual plunder which is eventually transformed into love, Gatsby tries to employ his idealizing capacity and imaginative response to beauty to transform the moral ugliness of this world.

Gatsby's story is full of contradictions. Enclosed within the glow of his own invented world, he is blind to both the corruption he seeks to realize in his dream and the impossibility of Daisy's ever measuring up to this vision of her.

The destruction of Gatsby's dream

In Chapter VIII, as the five of them drive aimlessly to New York, 'the relentless beating heat' is partly to be blamed for the mounting tension among them. In truth these tensions are chiefly generated by Gatsby's pressure on Daisy to act on the one hand, and by Tom's arrogance on the other. In urging Daisy to say that she never loved Tom, Gatsby proclaims that her life with Tom will all be 'wiped out forever' (p. 125). The word 'forever' has as little meaning in this context as when Nick uses it earlier. Gatsby's inability to appreciate that in the intervening years Daisy could have had an emotional life of her own marks his total commitment to his own dream rather than to Daisy herself. He feels physically assaulted by the idea that she should have loved Tom as well as himself.

'You loved me *too*?' he repeated. (p. 126)

When Tom asserts his social authority, Nick notes the expression on Gatsby's face – it was as if he had indeed 'killed a man' (p. 128). This is the first time Nick acknowledges to himself the shady nature of Gatsby's business connections, which would indeed require him to be tough, and concedes the possibility of some truth in the rumours. Nick's observation suggests that, if only momentarily, reality displaces the dream in Gatsby's mind. Yet the dream reasserts its hold, even if it is now only a 'dead dream' (p. 128), as Daisy draws away from Gatsby and Tom. The latter proves his power by permitting them to leave 'like ghosts' (p. 129). The dream, dead though it may be, determines Gatsby's identity by its hold over him while he waits outside Daisy's window for a signal. He remains the faithful lover, gazing at the lighted window representing the loved one. When Nick begins to describe Myrtle Wilson's death, Gatsby cannot bear to be reminded of her being ripped open, for such an intrusion by this kind of reality would destroy his image of Daisy.

Even as he and Nick talk through the night, his only thought is his all-consuming passion:

'I don't think she ever loved him.' . . .
'Of course she might have loved him just for a minute, when they were first married – and loved me more even then, do you see?' . . .
'In any case,' he said, 'it was just personal.' (pp. 144–5)

Nick invites the reader to share his bafflement:

What could you make of that, except to suspect some intensity in his conception of the affair that couldn't be measured? (p. 145)

Gatsby's love for Daisy is more than 'personal'. It is a passion permeating his entire life as well as his self-image. It is the depth of that feeling which holds Nick's fascination. By sustained patterns of imagery of light, colour and beauty, the style of narration pays tribute to the faithfulness with which Gatsby has held on to his image at the expense of rationality, the passing of time and any moral awareness, and this loyalty is maintained to the end. As he and Gatsby sit talking through the night, the dawn fills the house with 'grey-turning, gold-turning light' (p. 144) and 'ghostly birds began to sing among the blue leaves'. Gatsby's garden is still a 'blue' garden as it was on the nights of his parties but, significantly, the birdsong is ghostly now. Nick fills in the final details of Gatsby's despair at the loss of Daisy in 1919, when he journeyed to Louisville and found her memory there like a beatitude over the city where she had lived. When he left

... he knew that he had lost that part of it, the freshest and the best, forever. (p. 146)

Gatsby's dream of Daisy is connected with his youth and with a youthful vision of himself. Even in 1919 he knew that the best part of it had gone 'forever', but by an immense effort of will he clung to the dream, committing his whole life to it.

When Nick leaves, on impulse he calls across to Gatsby,

'They're a rotten crowd ... You're worth the whole damn bunch put together.' (p. 146)

As narrator he adds:

I've always been glad I said that. It was the only compliment I ever gave him, because I disapproved of him from beginning to end. (pp. 146-7)

Gatsby's moral identity still confuses and disturbs him.

Gatsby as victim

The sense of Gatsby as a sacrificial victim of society which Nick's description of the scene at the swimming-pool creates is intensified by the desertion of everyone connected with him in New York, by Daisy most of all.

Daisy doesn't send a message or a flower; Mr Gatz is bemused; Wolfshiem is sentimental; Klipspringer is already continuing his parasitical life elsewhere; one of the men who had enjoyed Gatsby's hospitality says he deserved all he got; Nick experiences the valley of ashes. Only Owl-eyes, the bespectacled guest at Gatsby's first party who showed an 'unusual quality of wonder' (p. 55), arrives to join him in the blessing of the dead and to add a modern benediction; he removes those corrective spectacles of the kind advertised by Doctor T. J. Eckleburg and speaks from the heart:

'Why, my God! they used to go there by the hundreds' ...
'The poor son-of-a-bitch,' he said. (p. 166)

This is the only time compassion is expressed in the entire novel. It is interesting that Fitzgerald puts it into the mouth of a minor character, an absurd figure from Gatsby's parties who was so drunk as to be a menace to himself and others. His reappearance and his inarticulacy sharpen the irony by controlling the emotion in the novel at this point.

There is an irony in the moral chaos and the confusion of all three deaths. George and Myrtle Wilson are victims too: Tom and Daisy are the survivors because they cheat and lie to save themselves. All the characters are interlinked in the very tight plotting: Gatsby is just as much an adulterer as Tom, and he contributes to the moral chaos of society by ruthlessly exploiting and breaking the law. Yet, by contrast to the others, Gatsby is faithful to a vision and he dies in its cause. The illusory nature of the vision is a source of irony, but it is a tragic irony.

The only character who is not caught in this web of ironically parallel and inter-connected relationships is Nick Carraway. He has a dual role in the novel: that of the observer standing on the sideline who, while drawn into a highly charged emotional situation in the summer of 1922, is still able to maintain intellectual and moral distance, and that of narrator one or two years later. His narration has to hold in balance his original sense of exploration and discovery, while at the same time presenting the insights that time and the experience itself have provided for him.

Nick Carraway

Nick is a Midwesterner whose aspiration to join the ranks of 'Midas and Morgan and Maecenas' (p. 10) takes him to New York, city of freedom and opportunity. Tom, Daisy, Jordan and Gatsby, who have all preceded him to the East, enjoy already the type of wealth to which, by implication, Nick is aspiring in his desire to benefit from those volumes standing on his shelf 'in red and gold like new money from the mint' (p. 10). 'In the meantime, in between time . . .' Nick, while on the threshold of Long Island society, is uncomfortably aware of the valley of ashes beside it. Like Gatsby, Nick is a newcomer to the world of vast wealth, and the social style of the very wealthy has its allure for him too. He has, after all, 'the consoling proximity of millionaires' (p. 11) to his shabby bungalow at West Egg.

Nick's 'journey' of discovery

Nick sees himself as 'a guide, a pathfinder, an original settler' (p. 9) when he has the opportunity of directing someone to West Egg village a day or so after moving in himself, having therefore achieved 'the freedom of the neighbourhood' (p. 9). The phrase itself has a certain ambiguity. Nonetheless, he remains a newcomer to the callous egotism and frivolity of Tom and Daisy's world. The East is a source of excitement to him: the city is 'almost pastoral' (p. 30). To his eager, exploring eye, it is 'like the blue honey of the Mediterranean' (p. 36); in his eyes, Gatsby's first party creates 'a sea-change of faces and voices and colour under the constantly changing light' (p. 42), and here 'sea-change' maintains the metaphor of voyaging. Nick begins to respond to the 'racy, adventurous feel' (p. 57) of New York at night and 'the satisfaction that the constant flicker of men and machines gives to the restless eye' (p. 57). His feeling of empathy with lonely young clerks wasting their lives until it was time for a solitary restaurant dinner (p. 57) is not necessarily as patronizing as some critics judge it to be. He is merely acknowledging the loneliness of life in a great modern city. His role of 'explorer' of modern city life is sustained when he crosses the Queensboro Bridge:

> The city seen from the Queensboro Bridge is always the city seen for the first time, in its first wild promise of all the mystery and the beauty in the world. (p. 67)

Nick's quality of imaginative wonder is an important feature of his capacity for empathy and his readiness to appreciate the full richness of life's variety in his quest for experience:

> I was within and without, simultaneously enchanted and repelled by the inexhaustible variety of life. (p. 37)

Unlike Nick, Gatsby is both dreamer and corrupt, unable to reconcile the two impulses or needs in himself: he cannot discriminate morally between the transfiguring vision of a unified self and the savage world of finance in which he seeks to express that self. Nick's narrative, on the other hand, written nearly two years after the experiences of 1922, assesses events by investing them with significance. To achieve such understanding turns out to have been the real goal of his journey of discovery. As narrator he shows himself able to share Gatsby's imaginative act of transforming the material world into 'the promise of all the mystery and the beauty in the world' (p. 67) while at the same time retaining a belief in the value of personal morality. He is both 'within' and 'without'. In the organization of the account of Nick's first journey to New York with Gatsby for example, on pp. 66–7, it is noteworthy that the abstract nouns 'mystery and beauty' follow immediately after Gatsby's display of his power with the police and precede their passing the hearse which serves as a reminder of death. Such a juxtaposition of details undercuts the original romanticism of his response to New York without, however, making it invalid.

Nick's role as observer and judge

Throughout his narrative Nick interposes comments and explanations, some of them sounding rather priggish or smug, about his own ethical identity, and it is sometimes difficult for the reader to recognize whether they represent Nick the immature participant in 1922 or Nick as subsequent more experienced narrator. At the beginning of the narrative he recalls his father's advice that a gentleman should practise tolerance. Although 'boasting this way' of tolerance, he points out that there is a limit to it, and only Gatsby is exempted from condemnation. Tolerance seems rather a cold attitude to adopt, implying detachment and disengagement from the plight of other people's lives, and it has led some readers to regard Nick as a prig.[9] But Nick's point seems to be that ethical principles (a brake on one's desires) are essential if one is to avoid inhabiting a world of indifferent chaos where the ego prevails and where people like Tom and Daisy smash 'things and creatures' (p. 170). After his confusion following the events of 1922, Nick now offers it as his considered judgement that Gatsby is to be admired for the series of gestures by which he remained loyal to his creative imagination, even to the extent of dying for it. Nick's measured judgements represent the way he has pondered upon Gatsby in the interim.

Initially in 1922 Nick appears to be passive and malleable, propelled by others as their guest, an uninvolved spectator in the first three social functions. In Chapter I, when dining with Tom and Daisy, he is pulled by Tom physically while both try to manipulate him emotionally: Tom turns him 'around by one arm' (p. 13), 'turned me around again' (p. 13), and 'compelled me' (p. 16); Daisy has a 'singing compulsion in her voice' (pp. 14–15) and uses it to 'compel my attention' (p. 22). During the disrupted dinner party Nick tries to 'avoid all eyes' (p. 21) and so is politely refusing to make any judgements. In Chapter II Tom insists that Nick meet his girl and 'his determination to have my company bordered on violence' (p. 27); during the evening, Nick feels entangled in arguments 'which pulled me back, as if with ropes' (p. 37), and when Myrtle points at him and says she was never more crazy about her husband than she was 'about that man there' (p. 37) he feels guilty, a moral outcast. In Chapter IV Gatsby calls on him:

'Good morning, old sport. You're having lunch with me today and I thought we'd ride up together.' (p. 62)

Nick seems to move on the edge of other people's lives at their whim or command. He tacitly accepts Jordan's murmured judgement to the effect that Daisy 'ought to have something in her life' (p. 77). This disengagement makes him an excellent narrator, but if their lives had had no relevance to his own moral or emotional experience the events of the novel would lack a core of significance. It is true that Nick names one moment of moral significance at an early point in the novel when Gatsby offers him a favour for services rendered; Nick could

pick up a nice bit of money. It happens to be a rather confidential sort of thing. (p. 80)

Presumably Nick would have been in the same position as Tom's friend Walter Chase, who served a month in jail for the connection (p. 127), or young Parke, who was picked up by the police (p. 158). As narrator Nick recalls:

I realize now that under different circumstances that conversation might have been one of the crises of my life. But, because the offer was obviously and tactlessly for a service to be rendered, I had no choice except to cut him off there. (p. 80)

Gatsby's offer lacks gentlemanly tact, and so Nick rejects it on the grounds of good taste or manners. He might otherwise have been corrupted by easy money. After all, there were many other young men who would show few scruples, like the young Englishmen at Gatsby's party.

I was sure that they were selling something: bonds or insurance or automobiles. They were at least agonizingly aware of the easy money in the vicinity and convinced that it was theirs for a few words in the right key. (p. 43)

The temptations of 'easy money' are manifold. However, Nick's ethical independence does not seem to have been really put to the test by Gatsby's offer, whether the manner of it offended his sensibility or not, and he remains on the fringe of the world of wealth, an aspiring novice within the legitimate boundaries of moneymaking, that is, stockbroking.

He informs the reader he likes 'to leave things in order' (p. 168). There is the girl back home with whom he has a certain 'understanding that had to be tactfully broken off before I was free' (p. 59). At this stage in his life tact appears to represent a personal ethic for Nick. There is the girl from Jersey City in the office, with whom he has a brief flirtation. His choice of language implies that she is socially inferior to himself, and when her brother takes an interest, he lets the relationship 'blow quietly away' (p. 57). Such language does not exactly endear him to the reader. Then there is Jordan Baker: when Nick begins to think himself in love with her he recalls his moral commitment to the girl at home.

But I am slow-thinking and full of interior rules that act as brakes on my desires. (p. 59)

The driving metaphor is deliberate, especially as it follows upon Nick's conversation with Jordan about careless driving – or egotism. Immediately after that he adds:

Everyone suspects himself of at least one of the cardinal virtues, and this is mine: I am one of the few honest people that I have ever known. (p. 59)

So far it would seem that Nick has been untouched and untried by experience, though he smugly assumes that this amounts to moral integrity. Even participation in the war has left no mark on him, since he 'enjoyed' (p. 9) it so thoroughly that it merely made him restless on his return home. Finally Nick makes an emotional commitment to Gatsby, which is later seen by him as a moral choice. He ultimately rejects Jordan because by maintaining complete detachment on the day of the New York trip she refuses to allow any emotional commitment to impinge upon her independence. In doing so, Nick rejects form and style as guiding principles: to merely observe the mores of a gentleman is not enough.

It is Nick's relationship with Gatsby in their roles of adventurer – pioneer – explorer – pathfinder – settler [10]– in the great modern commercial city and social hub of New York that constitutes his initiation into real ethical awareness. The contrary impulses that Gatsby experienced are Nick's also. In a letter Fitzgerald once defined the novel as 'a man's book', of 'purely masculine interest',[11] and though this judgement may seem to express a curiously limited appreciation of what interests women, it acknowledges the focus of attention in the novel, for the ethical problems confronted are those available only to men in the world of *making* money.

Compelled, even at the cost of his own moral aloofness and integrity, to play a role in the confused situation of despair, betrayal and death, Nick commits himself to a belief in Gatsby, fully aware though he is of the ugly facts of the dead man's corruption.

Nick as active participator

Once Gatsby is dead, Nick is forced to assume responsibility for him: as he takes the dead man's telephone calls he has almost, in a way, assumed Gatsby's identity. He even imagines what Gatsby must have experienced at the point of death. Consequently Nick moves to the centre of the narrative:

... it grew upon me that I was responsible, because no one else was interested – interested, I mean, with that intense personal interest to which everyone has some vague right at the end. (p. 156)

Nick rejects both Tom and Daisy's indifference and Gatsby's retreat into the solipsism of his dream. In telephoning Daisy 'instinctively and without hesitation' (p. 156) and trying to contact all the others, he is relying upon a common fund of feeling, not merely of decency, but of compassion – a sense that human life has a value, even in death. Their total lack of interest in Gatsby's death strikes him profoundly, the experience being so raw in his imagination that the East becomes a glittering and sophisticated wasteland 'distorted beyond my eyes' power of correction' (p. 167). It is Owl-eyes who blesses the dead man at Gatsby's lonely funeral, thereby expressing a synthesis of his awareness of Gatsby's life and compassion for him that Nick is too bitter to feel then. Time, the enemy of Gatsby's dream, is a necessary force in Nick's progress towards maturity and understanding.

At the end of his period in New York he 'broods' (p. 171) on the past – the expression deliberately evoking association with the blind eyes of Doctor T. J. Eckleburg brooding over the wasteland and seeing nothing. By contrast, Nick 'sees' some kind of continuity or pattern of experience in American history as well as in all human endeavour. His concluding vision of the unspoilt New World leads to the recognition that the ideal can never be more than an aspiration which is easily lost in the business of living in a complex and confusing world of material ambition.

The question remains whether Nick really comes to terms with his shattering experience of modern mores. In retreating home to the Midwest as a region in which old traditions and values have always seemed to offer him security in the past, he withdraws from the city which has challenged his sense of his own identity by its casting off of all moral constraints. It is easy enough for him to reject a way of life in which 'any little irregularity of your own' (p. 75) can be nicely timed for concealment, or consolation can be purchased in the form of 'a pearl necklace – or perhaps only a pair of cuff buttons' (p. 170). It is Gatsby who is the crux of Nick's problem, because he is Nick's alter ego who succumbed to the power of wealth to construct a world of beauty of his own devising. Nick's concluding insights offer a synthesis of the wasteland and the beautiful dream within a perspective of life. His role as narrator offers the real evidence – in the way he brilliantly maintains the two in equilibrium: he has opted for the power of words to construct a world, not the power of wealth.

Conclusion

Nick Carraway and Scott Fitzgerald, writers of 'this book' (p. 8)

Fitzgerald allows Nick to claim authorship of the book. At one point Nick is 'Reading over what I have written so far' (p. 56) and commenting on his own reporting of the events of that summer. Fitzgerald thus rejects the role of omniscient author by allowing the personality of Gatsby to emerge seemingly at random through the contingencies of Nick's life in New York and through Nick's perceptions. Events which Nick did not – and could not – witness are reconstructed from others' accounts and retold by him. By this means, Nick's mind and ethical crisis are ultimately made the focus of the narrative. His blend of imaginative excitement and ironic detachment hold in balanced tension the two ways of perceiving the world through which the narrative is structured. For example, at first Nick 'sees' Gatsby's parties largely in the terms which Gatsby, like a magician, has created – but never entirely, for he remains alert to all the hard work by the servants in preparing them and clearing the ravages afterwards. Similarly, Nick appreciates the enchantment that Tom Buchanan's wealth can command, but he is alive to the moral failures concealed beneath it. As Nick's initial glowing images are modulated, the equally distorting wasteland of egotism seems to become paramount for him, at least in his nightmares. Ultimately, his synthesis of the wasteland and the dream ends the novel.

The writing, of course, is Fitzgerald's. In the course of painting a bleak picture of the attitudes and feelings apposite to the Jazz Age, he developed a brilliant style of writing wholly appropriate for exploring the nature of reality in the contemporary world of the United States, which was rapidly assuming the role and status of the leading financial power in the world.

6. America: History and Myth

The title of the novel

The problem of choosing a title for the novel presented some difficulty before publication. In November 1924 Fitzgerald wrote to his editor:

> I have now decided to stick to the title I put on the book. *Trimalchio in West Egg*. The only other titles that seem to fit are *Trimalchio* and *On the Road to West Egg*. I had two others, *Gold-Hatted Gatsby* and *The High-Bouncing Lover*, but they seemed too light.[1]

Trimalchio was a wealthy upstart in ancient Rome as portrayed in a satire by the Roman writer Petronius. Such a choice of title would have emphasized Gatsby's status as social outsider, but it would also have directed attention to a parallel outside America. The last two suggestions relate to the epigraph Fitzgerald wrote under the jokey pseudonym Thomas Parke D'Invilliers.[2] Daisy's delight as she fingers Gatsby's toilet set of pure dull gold (p. 89) perhaps comes nearest to expressing this, since she is certainly aware of him as 'gold-hatted' and is on the point of taking Gatsby as her lover again, in effect saying, 'I must have you!' In the event, none of these titles was selected.

Fitzgerald never cared for the title finally settled upon, which was his editor's preference, and he afterwards blamed it for the commercial failure of the novel.[3] A few weeks before publication he cabled his editor from Paris suggesting an alternative title, *Under the Red, White and Blue*, but it was too late to make such a change. His proposal presumably picks up the reference to the national flags flying during the war (p. 72) and was intended perhaps to reflect ironically on the American scene. It would have stressed cogently the images of American history and identity which permeate the novel, labelling the story as an essentially American one and stressing the ironic implications of its treatment of contemporary America.

Within the period covering the events in the novel, those few summer months in New York in 1922, Fitzgerald incorporated significant references to the American past and to another region where there still persisted traditions and values different from those of wealthy New York socialites and show business people in the Jazz Age. In his role of narrator, Nick – who, like all the main characters, is a Midwesterner drawn to the East coast by the lure of the city asserting its twentieth-century status as the centre of an exciting and liberated new culture – makes several contrasts between the two regions, East Coast and Midwest. While Nick may over-simplify the contrast in its moral terms, the tenor of the novel conveys the whole American past as a continuous process in which idealism and the pursuit of material goals are intertwined. American identity is a central concern of the novel, and no other proposed titles express this so clearly as Fitzgerald's final suggestion would have done. The published title does not appear to do so either, but I shall argue that Gatsby's 'greatness' is set within the American tradition. He is an essentially American figure. The rather puzzling title focuses on Gatsby as the central figure of interest. It also appears to elevate him to legendary status as heroic, a memorable or 'great' personage who expressed his personality in a 'series of successful gestures'.

This is probably the lasting impression retained by many readers, and it is the one deliberately sought by the artistic structuring of the novel. It is also given credence by the lack of detail concerning the way Gatsby amassed such fabulous wealth. But there is also, however, an element of irony and paradox in the title, for Gatsby's fortune was founded on an illicit, possibly criminal, exploitation of the post-war scene and a willingness to ignore ethical considerations. It is Nick's role to represent the point of ethical reference, yet it is Gatsby with his dream who stirs the reader's imagination. By his handling of the central character, Fitzgerald makes Gatsby's life something of a contemporary myth; he becomes an American figure incorporating elements of the strands of impulse, aspiration and identity which make up a major national myth, and the title directs the reader's attention towards this aspect. In this chapter I shall examine some national and historical dimensions of the 'myth of America' in terms of its past, the characters of Meyer Wolfshiem and Tom Buchanan as co-heirs of that past, and the significant use of American landscape in the novel.

Myth as history

Nick's experiences not only parallel in important ways Gatsby's story, they also add new levels of meaning to it through the different time perspectives they offer in the narrative structure. Nick's final vision both re-enacts Gatsby's rapt gaze across the Sound to the green light on Daisy's dock *and* draws together other images of landscape and time which also represent psychological states. His vision is given climactic significance by its position at the end of the novel as well as by the tone and cadences of the prose, and for this reason I shall quote it extensively. In 'seeing' a mythical moment of American history, Nick finds in it a peculiarly American hope and regret for the unattainable dream. This is the crux of Gatsby's identity, which Nick defines at the beginning of the novel as his 'heightened sensitivity to the promises of life . . . an extraordinary gift for hope' (p. 8).

p. 171

. . . gradually I became aware of the old island here that flowered once for Dutch sailors' eyes – a fresh green breast of the new world. Its vanished trees, the trees that had made way for Gatsby's house, had once pandered in whispers to the last and greatest of all human dreams; for a transitory enchanted moment man must have held his breath in the presence of this continent, compelled into an aesthetic contemplation he neither understood nor desired, face to face for the last time in history with something commensurate to his capacity for wonder.

Nick's glimpse of a founding moment of the American nation and its destiny has a paradoxical quality. Despite the profit motive which sent them out across the Atlantic ocean to these distant and unknown shores, the men are caught in an intense emotional experience. The imagery of 'flowered' and 'fresh green breast' endows the experience with concepts of growth, nourishment, beauty, gentleness and natural bounty – traditional female characteristics. The newly discovered land has not yet been deflowered or ravaged or exploited for profit. Yet such associations are countered by 'pandered', which suggests procuring. The men's dream of a new world which might nourish a new way of life is a delusion, for the moment was enchanted, outside the reality of time. History is concerned with material expansion and profit, and their 'aesthetic' vision could not be sustained against the course of modern history. Yet 'aesthetic' implies a response of the spirit or imagination to a beauty which creates order and harmony. While Nick's vision invests those sailors of the seventeenth century, sent out from one of the leading trading nations of Europe, with a capacity for such personal feeling, it also admits that history and individual desire combined to frustrate it.

The language and imagery of flowers, light and sea link this moment of heightened experience shared by Nick and those imagined sailors with Gatsby's dream of Daisy. The alternative world of the valley of ashes is also drawn into the web of meaning as an implied contrast, for the Dutch sailors' eyes are not lifeless signs like the painted eyes of Doctor T. J. Eckleburg (p. 26): they respond with a surge of emotion to the primal beauty of the Long Island shore, which three hundred years later will have been transformed into an industrial-urban wasteland. Idealism and hope are an essential ingredient of American history, but they have been frustrated regularly by the more powerful forces of material desire, just as they are in Gatsby's experience. Gatsby is thus transformed by Nick and by the narrative method into a representative figure of American destiny who dreams of realizing an idealizing vision in an ecstatic ('orgastic')[4] future. Ironically, however, young James Gatz's first awed response to beauty was centred on Dan Cody's yacht. Through Cody, Gatsby is linked to the nineteenth-century pioneering expansion westwards, which in turn enabled the exploitation of vast mineral reserves to create American industrial capital, and the first millionaires too. Modern American power and wealth were established by aggressive exploitation of such natural resources by some real-life Cody figures.

In Chapter VIII (pp. 141–5), Gatsby fills in some details of his earlier life for Nick, who, as narrator, has already anticipated these disclosures (pp. 94–7), following Gatsby's reunion with Daisy. Young James Gatz's meeting with millionaire Dan Cody, portrayed as a leading figure of modern American capitalism, transformed both his life and his identity. The analysis is Nick's, not Gatsby's.

pp. 94–7

Cody was fifty years old then, a product of the Nevada silver fields, of the Yukon,[5] of every rush for metal since seventy-five. The transactions in Montana copper that made him many times a millionaire found him physically robust but on the verge of soft-mindedness ...

I remember the portrait of him up in Gatsby's bedroom, a grey, florid man with a hard, empty face – the pioneer debauchee, who during one phase of American life brought back to the Eastern seaboard the savage violence of the frontier brothel and saloon ...

Nick's language represents an indictment of Cody and his life. When young James Gatz found favour with this dissipated, prematurely ageing millionaire in his yacht on Lake Superior, he

invented just the sort of Jay Gatsby that a seventeen-year-old boy would be likely to invent

to fit himself for a new life. Cody's yacht, the *Tuolemee*, has been variously identified as named after the goldmines of California or of Alaska.[6] It is clear that Fitzgerald intended the episode to relate significantly to American history during the expansion of the frontier westwards and the accumulation of great wealth. Dan Cody's name may have association with two historical figures of the nineteenth century who became almost legendary heroes of frontier life, Daniel Boone and William Cody. Both were popularized in their own lifetimes in stories and novels, the latter becoming widely known as Buffalo Bill with his

Critical Studies: The Great Gatsby

Wild West Show.[7] While Dan Cody's name may identify him with frontiersmen who caught the nation's imagination through stories of individual daring, his role as a founding father of modern wealth at the same time put an end to that wild, free frontier life.

Much has been written in recent years of the Frontier, both as a major theme of American history and as a myth of the seemingly limitless opportunities offered by the vast, unknown American continent waiting to be conquered and developed – a myth which operated as a powerful stimulus to the American imagination. Ever since the first settlers voyaged to the Eastern seaboard to begin a new life, the New World presented a place of hope – a dream – and an unknown interior of vast proportions awaiting claimants: it represented

that dream of a land in which life should be better and richer and fuller for every man, with opportunity for each according to his ability and achievement.[8]

The possibility of new beginnings continued to be epitomized by the Frontier as it was extended westwards towards the Pacific coast. In 1839, an American journal announced with an extraordinary degree of high-flown rhetoric:

The expansive future is our arena, and for our history. We are entering on its untrodden space.

. . . We are the nation of human progress, and who will, what can, set limits to our onward march? . . . The far-reaching, the boundless future will be the arena of American greatness. In its magnificent domain of space and time, the nation of many nations is destined to manifest the excellence of divine principles.[9]

In *The Great Gatsby*, Dan Cody, who had amassed his fortune under the most brutalizing circumstances, rejected all such divine principles and along with them the encumbrance of social ties or responsibilities, as well as the constraints of an ethical code. His yacht symbolizes a link with the recurrent imagery of sea-voyaging, but it is significant that Cody sailed around the American continent three times in his premature old age. His circling it can be seen as metaphorically imprisoning the nation, entrapping it within his predatory opportunism, closing it to a wide range of possibilities. In the same way his morality of 'the savage violence of the frontier brothel and saloon' (p. 97) contributed to a sexual ethic linked inextricably with money, which contributed to the wasteland of the valley of ashes where men like George Wilson are reduced to the status of ghosts. Cody would seem to be the antithesis of the American dream, yet in fact he also represents its other aspect, the goal of wealth and success. Any dream which appears to offer so much to so many must of necessity be ambiguous. Gatsby, too, was craving

for wealth and success, but he is not Cody's true heir, for he
primarily as a means to attaining an idealized self, not as en
selves.

In Chapter IX Gatsby's bemused father says of his dead so

'If he'd of lived, he'd of been a great man. A man like James J. Hill. He'd of
helped build up the country.' (p. 160)

There was a real James J. Hill who rose from poor boy to railroad
magnate in the Midwest. In support of his assertion Mr Gatz brings out
of his pocket, along with a photograph of his son's house, symbol of
success in his eyes, a 'ragged old copy of a book called *Hopalong
Cassidy*'[10] (p. 164). Like the fictionalized heroes that Daniel Boone and
William Cody were turned into, Hopalong Cassidy was a popular fictional
version of the frontiersman, the lone cowboy who rides the range meting
out justice, a figure soon to be portrayed in whole series of cowboy
films. Fitzgerald brings together a cluster of meanings and associations
in the episode when Mr Gatz proudly shows Nick young Jimmy's
schoolboy schedule and resolutions, written on the inside cover of his
copy of the novel and dated September 12, 1906:

'It just shows you, don't it?' . . .
'Jimmy was bound to get ahead.' (p. 164)

For the reader there is both pathos and poignancy in these schoolboy
resolutions, particularly at this point in the novel when Gatsby lies in
lonely death. The 'Schedule' and 'General Resolves' are also ludicrous,
as Nick well knows. Fitzgerald achieves a level of ironic implication in
this by placing the scene at this point in the narrative. Yet Jimmy Gatz's
schoolboy ambition, together with Mr Gatz's naïve admiration for
success, aligns Gatsby with a number of historical figures who gained a
deep hold on the American imagination, contributing to the dream of
'getting ahead' as a goal which all might share in a land which valued
enterprise. The spirit of individual effort and enterprise is an important
constituent of the national identity and Gatsby's subsequent career is in
many ways an exemplification of this.[11] In the war he rose to the rank of
major, his bravery was recognized officially, and he was rewarded with
the chance to mingle with the landed aristocracy of England at 'Oggsford'
(p. 70). To what extent his business partnership with Wolfshiem was on
the wrong side of the law is never made clear. Modern commercial
practice often confuses the line of demarcation, and Fitzgerald may have
deliberately blurred this issue in order to make Gatsby a contemporary
exponent of the rags to riches story.

Young Jimmy Gatz's youthful resolves are very much in the tradition of advice given by a leading American figure in the eighteenth century, Benjamin Franklin, who made a fortune as a printer by hard work and enterprise before becoming a diplomat. He produced a publication called *Poor Richard's Almanack*, advocating self-help as the best course of action for ambitious young men, and misspelt and inadequate though they may be, the 'Schedule' and 'General Resolves' are conceived in this tradition. Another popular writer who endorsed the notion that effort is in itself a virtue that will be rewarded by wealth and success was Horatio Alger. Through charitable work in the late nineteenth century, he came to know something of the ragged street boys of New York before proceeding to sentimentalize the theme of getting ahead in a series of popular novels. It has been said of Alger that he 'left a deeper mark on American character than the works of many a greater mind!'[12]

In seizing his destiny Gatsby epitomizes the ethic of individual enterprise in a land of boundless opportunities, but there is a savage irony in Fitzgerald's portrayal of the nature of his success in an age which on the one hand cast off the constraints of the past and on the other saw the emergence of modern society enjoying wealth on a previously unimaginable scale. But Gatsby is an ambivalent figure whom Nick puzzles over during much of the narrative, just as the American dream is ambivalent in its optimistic ideal of new beginnings inseparable from the goal of material success. In Gatsby, Fitzgerald portrays a split in the American psyche produced by the action of American history. Gatsby is a divided personality, ambivalent even in his death, and the structure of the narrative, in particular the way it concentrates on his moments of intense emotional experience, insists upon this ambivalence.

Gatsby's entrepreneurial activities between 1919 and 1922 – which transformed him from a penniless and hungry young ex-soldier into the owner of a baronial hall on Long Island, a hydroplane and a magnificent car – are merely hinted at. Instead, the narrative concentrates on those moments of heightened subjective experience which gave him a glimpse of an ideal self. His moment of ecstasy when he kissed Daisy in 1917 is described by Nick in these terms.

pp. 106–7

. . . the sidewalk was white with moonlight . . . The quiet lights in the houses were humming out into the darkness and there was a stir and bustle among the stars. Out of the corner of his eye Gatsby saw that the blocks of the sidewalks really formed a ladder and mounted to a secret place above the trees – he could climb to it, if he climbed alone, and once there he could suck on the pap of life, gulp down the incomparable milk of wonder.

Gatsby's ladder does not point to conventional economic success, for it directs him towards an idealized self.

At his lips' touch she blossomed for him like a flower and the incarnation was complete.

For him Daisy incarnates his dream, her presence being the physical expression of it, which will give substance to his identity as Jay Gatsby, yet Daisy herself, always surrounded and cosseted by the accoutrements of wealth, is a product of her upbringing and luxurious environment. Like the American Dream, the meaning of Gatsby's dream remains ambivalent. It always was, for it was Dan Cody who turned up in Little Girl Bay as Jimmy Gatz's 'destiny', and it was Cody's yacht that afforded him his first glimpse of 'all the beauty and glamour in the world' (p. 96). Significantly, the photographs of Cody and the yacht are the only mementoes of his past that Gatsby keeps on display in his bedroom. Daisy misreads the signs and estimates his status accordingly.

'I adore it,' exclaimed Daisy. 'The pompadour! You never told me you had a pompadour – or a yacht.' (p. 90)

His idealizing dream can never be divorced from the wealth which history has created. He cannot transcend the American past or step aside from historical time. He becomes a figure of tragic intensity helplessly enmeshed in his environment and contributing to its ugliness even while he is creating an evanescent beauty in order to try to transcend it. Gatsby is 'great' in his role as representative contemporary hero corrupted by new opportunities for wealth, yet aspiring to escape their consequences by investing money with a private radiance generated by his imagination.[13] Accordingly, the language and imagery Fitzgerald employs attribute a luminous but fragile beauty to the landscape of wealth Gatsby creates, while at the same time linking him to the wasteland.

The heirs of Dan Cody: Meyer Wolfshiem and Tom Buchanan

Heir to a slice of Dan Cody's fortune, Gatsby was tricked out of his inheritance by Ella Kaye. In the novel the true heirs to the world of wealth Cody created and the ethics by which he did so are Meyer Wolfshiem and Tom Buchanan. Wolfshiem employs a more sophisticated version of Cody's crude style, while Tom Buchanan's wealth is now graced by social acceptability. Both are national figures in their own way. While Gatsby is fully implicated in Wolfshiem's activities, he

...them as a means to the achievement of his incorruptible dream ...will give him his 'true' identity. Wolfshiem and Tom are quite ...t with the identities they possess, and in some respects constitute ... caricature representatives of greed and power. The portrayal of both is savagely satirical in its implications.

Wolfshiem's name brands him as a creature of prey, and there is an additional suggestion of the carnivore in the detail of his much-prized cuff-links:

'Finest specimens of human molars,' he informed me. (p. 70)

When Nick is introduced to him in a New York restaurant in Chapter IV, the plaster Presbyterian nymphs on the ceiling are mere onlookers, futile reminders of the old-established Puritan ethic once paramount in New England as a force moulding American identity. But traditionally nymphs are scantily dressed figures enjoying sexual freedom, and the message seems to be that the old ethic has lost its power in modern, sexually and ethically emancipated New York. Under the impression that Nick is looking for 'a business gonnegtion' (p. 69), Wolfshiem talks expansively in front of him about his own business methods. While he may sound comic, he clearly wields sufficient power to terrify people and silence opposition.

'I handed the money to Katspaugh and I said: "All right, Katspaugh, don't pay him a penny till he shuts his mouth." He shut it then and there.' (p. 68)

Later, during the disastrous trip to New York in Chapter VII, Tom reveals the nature of Wolfshiem's and Gatsby's business activities.

'He and this Wolfshiem bought up a lot of side-street drug-stores here and in Chicago and sold grain alcohol over the counter.' (p. 127)

Tom's friend Walter Chase has already served a jail sentence for his connection with Wolfshiem, and even now could get him and Gatsby into trouble for impinging the betting laws, 'but Wolfshiem scared him into shutting his mouth' (p. 128). Wolfshiem employs gangster methods, but it was when he 'fixed the World's Series back in 1919' (p. 71) that he showed his real entrepreneurial genius. Nick is astounded:

... if I had thought of it at all I would have thought of it as a thing that merely *happened*, the end of some inevitable chain. It never occurred to me that one man could start to play with the faith of fifty million people – (p. 71)

'He just saw the opportunity', is how Gatsby explains it.

Just as Ella Kaye betrayed the meaning of sexual relationships in appropriating Dan Cody's entire fortune after his death, so Wolfshiem betrays friendship when he is unable to attend Gatsby's funeral because he's 'tied up in some very important business and cannot get mixed up in this thing now' (p. 157). When Nick forces his way into Wolfshiem's office, Gatsby's erstwhile partner declares that once a man gets killed he never likes to get 'mixed' up in the matter (p. 163). True to form, he sentimentalizes his past business connection with Gatsby, recalling the days of their early partnership when the younger man was newly demobbed, jobless and hungry.

'Start him! I made him.' (p. 162)

He continues:

'I raised him up out of nothing, right out of the gutter. I saw right away he was a fine-appearing, gentlemanly young man, and when he told me he was at Oggsford I knew I could use him good. I got him to join the American legion and he used to stand high there. Right off he did some work for a client of mine up to Albany.' (p. 162)

Wolfshiem makes it sound like the road to success through honest effort and industry, but it may be presumed that Gatsby's connection with the Legion, an organization for ex-soldiers, was exploited for very dubious ends.

Wolfshiem's reminiscences in Chapter IV about his association with Rosy Rosenthal before the latter was gunned down outside 'the old Metropole' connect him with the historical figures and events mentioned in Chapter 1 of this study. A notable presence in the world of crime, he is totally implicated in corruption. He is more sinister than those persons with criminal connections in the list compiled by Nick of Gatsby's guests that summer. Wolfshiem represents the underside of the wealth, spontaneity and vitality generated by New York in the Jazz Age. His world holds no apparent concourse with the privileged set of Tom Buchanan, but the desire of Tom's friend Walter Chase to 'pick up some money' (p. 128) indicates that they are not totally unconnected. Since Tom has no trouble in investigating Gatsby's financial affairs, he is not so remote from them as might be imagined. He is simply more socially exclusive.

Tom Buchanan, like Daisy, belongs to an older-established world of wealth. As he comes from Chicago it is likely that he is descended from the great meat-packing families establishing themselves there towards the end of the last century.[14] In Chapter I Nick recalls:

His family were enormously wealthy – even in college his freedom with money was a matter for reproach – but now he'd left Chicago and come East in a fashion that rather took your breath away: for instance, he'd brought down a string of polo ponies from Lake Forest. It was hard to realize that a man in my own generation was wealthy enough to do that. (p. 11)

On the night before he married Daisy 'with more pomp and circumstance than Louisville ever knew before' . . . 'he gave her a string of pearls valued at three hundred and fifty thousand dollars' (p. 74). These pearls of great price visibly proclaim Daisy's social value as his wife.

Tom himself has no doubts about the social value of his house on the fashionable Long Island shore.

'It belonged to Demaine, the oil man.' (p. 13)

That is all he needs to say to locate its place in the social hierarchy. Tom's view of society is totally hierarchical, his own position by established right being at the top. There is irony in his fears for the decline of civilization, since his brutal arrogance and complete lack of moral concern are a measure of that decline in the novel. Though possessing all the physical energy that might once have sent him out like Cody on 'every rush for metal', he has no outlet now.

> Not even the effeminate swank of his riding clothes could hide the enormous power of his body – he seemed to fill those glistening boots until he strained the top lacing, and you could see a great pack of muscle shifting when his shoulder moved under his thin coat. It was a body capable of enormous leverage – a cruel body. (p. 12)

This memorable description effectively implants Tom in the reader's imagination, the emphasis on barely restrained physical power denoting his mental attitude. Now that he no longer has the football field in which to assert himself, he exercises his need for power in a sexual way. A tense man, barely able to contain his violent tendencies even at the dinner party in Chapter I, he suddenly introduces a bizarre note into the conversation.

> 'Civilization's going to pieces,' broke out Tom violently. 'I've gotten to be a terrible pessimist about things. Have you read *The Rise of the Coloured Empires* by this man Goddard?' [15]
> . . . 'Well, it's a fine book, and everybody ought to read it. The idea is if we don't look out the white race will be – will be utterly submerged . . .'
> '. . . This fellow has worked out the whole thing. It's up to us, who are the dominant race, to watch out or these other races will have control of things.' (p. 18)

Nick finds Tom's intellectual efforts to expound the half-baked ideas he has picked up rather pathetic. What Tom is reproducing here are repulsive theories buttressing his own sense of racial and cultural superiority. Tom is a bully whose every word echoes his sense of innate superiority.

Tom's wealth prevents him from pursuing any course of action by which he might express a meaningful identity. He is a representative figure of the leisured class, produced in an earlier age by such adventurers as Dan Cody, whose life now lacks fulfilment. Tom's eyes flash about restlessly as he speaks, and he and Daisy have

drifted here and there unrestfully, wherever people played polo and were rich together. (p. 11)

But Tom is particularly repulsive in the way he is blind to the truth about himself. He adopts a tone of moral censure about the new freedom enjoyed by women, which he suspects of undermining the paternalism he assumes towards women of his own class. Jordan Baker's family 'oughtn't to let her run around the country this way' (p. 23). The irony of his double standards is clear, since the call from his 'woman in New York' (p. 20) and Daisy's story about Tom being 'God knows where' (p. 22) when their daughter was born have already conveyed some of his moral attitudes towards family life. During Gatsby's second party in Chapter VI, Tom happily joins another group where 'a fellow's getting off some funny stuff' (p. 102), but Daisy, knowing his tastes, reports that the girl is 'common but pretty'. Yet Tom is put out at the thought that Daisy should even have met Gatsby socially.

'. . . By God, I may be old-fashioned in my ideas, but women run around too much these days to suit me. They meet all kinds of crazy fish.' (p. 100)

When Tom summons all his social authority to crush Gatsby in Chapter VII, he declares that Gatsby could never have got within a mile of Daisy in 1917, 'unless you brought the groceries to the back door' (p. 125), and he triumphantly reduces Gatsby's love to a 'presumptuous little flirtation' (p. 129).

Tom Buchanan is by far the most unpleasant character in a novel already containing a number of unattractive characters. He possesses power and great wealth without responsibilities. Enjoying the status of a grand seigneur in an aristocratic state, he is nonetheless uncommitted to any code of ethics. This is evident in his relationship with Myrtle Wilson, or with the chambermaid who was hurt in the car accident. In telling how her affair with Tom began, Myrtle makes it clear that part of his appeal was his 'dress suit and patent leather shoes' (p. 38), the mark of a gentleman in her eyes. She just couldn't keep her eyes off him, for the visible signs of his status were an added lure.

At the end of the novel, Nick feels as if he were talking to a child: Tom is so entrenched in his self-righteousness and his sense of class superiority that he is impervious to any other considerations. He feels quite justified in having given George Wilson Gatsby's address when he was fully aware of what Wilson would do. Other people's tragedies make no impression on him, and in any case he is convinced that he has had his 'share of suffering' in the situation. Nick last glimpses him entering a Fifth Avenue jeweller's 'to buy a pearl necklace – or perhaps only a pair of cuff buttons' (p. 170). Tom is unscathed, protected by his immense wealth from any form of self-awareness other than a social one. Impregnable in the wealth and millionaire status that Cody and his kind established, Tom can make his own rules while denying other people any independent reality.

In a short story called 'Rich Boy'[16] which Fitzgerald published the following year, the narrator comments: 'Let me tell you about the very rich. They are different from you and me.' The difference in Fitzgerald's view is in their sense of inalienable right to what they possess. Like the prematurely ageing Dan Cody once he had amassed his fortune, Tom drifts purposelessly through life. Gratification of desire, together with an exaggerated sense of his own status, is all that concerns him. The frontier that once provided the promise of an expansive future no longer exists, but there is no sense of community to replace it. Compared with either Tom or Wolfshiem, Gatsby is aligned with older American ideals because he

... believed in the green light, the orgastic future that year by year recedes before us ... (p. 171)

Nick points out that Gatsby

did not know that it was already behind him, somewhere back in that vast obscurity beyond the city, where the dark fields of the republic rolled on under the night. (p. 171)

The 'dark fields of the republic' include the West and Midwest, where Dan Cody and Tom and Daisy's families acquired the fortunes that gave enormous wealth such an allure. The whole nation is implicated in the wealth in which New York now glitters.

Symbolic landscapes: Midwest and East coast

In his role as 'writer' of the book, Nick Carraway establishes his credentials as narrator of Gatsby's story by deliberately focusing the Midwest as a region possessing a moral identity which shaped his life. Again and again in the novel he contrasts it with the sophisticated East. His initial account makes the territory in which he grew up a centre of old-established values, while New York is made representative of the twentieth-century morals and culture which express contemporary America. His brief autobiographical sketch merits examination.

pp. 8–9

My family have been prominent, well-to-do people in this Middle Western city[17] for three generations. The Carraways are something of a clan, and we have a tradition that we're descended from the Dukes of Buccleuch, but the actual founder of my line was my grandfather's brother, who came here in fifty-one, sent a substitute to the Civil War, and started the wholesale hardware business that my father carries on today.

I never saw this great-uncle, but I'm supposed to look like him – with special reference to the rather hard-boiled painting that hangs in father's office. I graduated from New Haven in 1915,[18] just a quarter of a century after my father, and a little later I participated in that delayed Teutonic migration known as the Great War. I enjoyed the counter-raid so thoroughly that I came back restless. Instead of being the warm centre of the world, the Middle West now seemed like the ragged edge of the universe – so I decided to go East and learn the bond business. Everybody I knew was in the bond business, so I supposed it could support one more single man. All my aunts and uncles talked it over as if they were choosing a prep school for me, and finally said, 'Why – ye-es,' with very grave, hesitant faces. Father agreed to finance me for a year, and after various delays I came East, permanently, I thought, in the spring of twenty-two.

The Middle West is thus invested with stability. Nick's family is a cohesive unit, with its traditional hierarchy of aunts and uncles who all share authority over the young. The family has a history of three generations, a past – probably legendary rather than real – associating it with European aristocracy, representing the sense of continuity that led Nick to follow his father to Yale. It endorses the code of ethics summed up on p. 7 as 'a sense of the fundamental decencies', in other words, the traditional codes proper to a lady or a gentleman.

Yet Nick's family history in the Midwest contains something of an anomaly. The family business was established at the time of the American Civil War (1861–5), a major conflict between Northern and Southern states on the issue of slavery, which was fought on both sides with great courage and passion on grounds of principle and honour. However, the founder of Nick's family's prosperity took no part in the war but sent a substitute while he got on with the matter of establishing a profitable concern.

A recent critic[19] notes that the sum of three hundred dollars for the hire of a substitute could purchase remission from military service. Self-interest and commercial caution, rather than idealism, set up Nick's 'prominent, well-to-do' family in a life-style which allowed them to observe a code of honour and to appear in 1922 to epitomize values far removed from those of New York. Nick offers no comment on this, but the fact that he mentions this at all suggests a scepticism regarding the existence of such a simple dichotomy as this between the two regions.

Yet it is for this reason that Nick returns to the Midwest as a refuge after the events in New York. He sketches his state of mind at that time in the beginning of the narrative:

When I came back . . . last autumn I felt that I wanted the world to be in uniform and at a sort of moral attention forever; I wanted no more riotous excursions with privileged glimpses into the human heart. (p. 8)

Such language arouses the reader's expectations about what is to follow, but moreover it suggests that Nick was seeking to escape from the traumas just experienced. The word 'forever' has no validity, especially when it is involved as a formula for making life stand still in order to avoid the pain of harsh experience. Nick concludes this particular passage by confessing that his interest in 'the abortive sorrows and short-winded elations of men had only been temporarily' closed out. The implication is that in the interim (in the meantime, in between time), he has attained a stage of maturity enabling him to judge matters in a more considered way, for now he believes that 'Reserving judgements is a matter of infinite hope' (p. 7). His journey to the sophisticated East, however painfully it turned out, has proved a journey towards maturity. Nick's opening set of confidences in fact links the two regions in a more complex relationship than is at first apparent.

Nick's discriminations are resumed at the end of the novel. While referring to his decision to return home (p. 167), he reminisces about his boyhood.

One of my most vivid memories is of coming back West from prep school and later from college at Christmas time. (p. 166)

He remembers scenes of friendships, security, Christmas festivities, long train journeys across great continental stretches of land, but these 'memories' seem to have become transmuted into magical, unreal experiences in the way that often happens when the remembered scene becomes an idyll.

That's my Middle West . . . the thrilling returning trains of my youth. (p. 167)

Leaving the Union Street station in Chicago they used to traverse the Chicago, Milwaukee and St Paul railroad on the long journey across the snow-covered plains of Wisconsin and Minnesota. Nick cherishes what is essentially a Christmas card vision of a vanished world of childhood and innocence epitomized by streetlamps, sleighbells and the shadows of holly wreaths cast on the snow. He endows memories of this Midwest, filtered through the glow of nostalgia, with a moral superiority over the disorienting East which has undermined his sense of his own identity. 'His' glowing Midwest reflects his psychological need for a stable, comprehensible and secure world, and after Gatsby's death he tries to make it a reality.

Nick confesses that since Gatsby's death New York has become a source of nightmare which has disturbed him from the first even while it excited him.

> Even when the East excited me most, even when I was most keenly aware of its superiority to the bored sprawling, swollen towns beyond the Ohio, with their interminable inquisitions which spared only the children and the very old – even then it had always for me a quality of distortion. (p. 167)

New York offers freedom from the constraints and irritations of family life in the provinces, but it is at the same time a worrying liberation for a young man like Nick, not least in the new status it accords to women.

> West Egg, especially, still figures in my more fantastic dreams. I see it as a nightmare scene by El Greco:[20] a hundred houses, at once conventional and grotesque, crouching under a sullen, overhanging sky and a lustreless moon. (p. 167)

He goes on to record his nightmare of the drunken woman which has been analysed in Chapter 4 of this study, the language echoing but distorting the images used in depicting Gatsby's parties in Chapter II in order to evoke a nightmare scene of decadence and alienation.

Nick knows that his personal nightmare distorts and exaggerates the moral chaos of the East, but at the time of Gatsby's death he lacks the capacity to achieve a balanced perspective, for his view of life is 'distorted beyond my eyes' power of correction' (p. 167). He is haunted by the recent past, unlike Gatsby, who was a man haunted by a dream of the future. Fitzgerald employs this nightmare vision artistically to create the patterning web of images of night and moonlight which constitute both Gatsby's and Nick's deepest experiences. East and West become synthesized in the imagery of light and beauty. Gatsby's moments of transcendent feeling were centred on Louisville and the young Daisy, but he projected them into the green light across the bay on Long Island. Nick finally perceives in the East a continuing source of hope for American destiny, even though he is on the point of retreat to the Midwest when he does so.[21]

The framing device of Nick's presence as narrator, together with the fact that he, Gatsby, Tom, Daisy and Jordan are all young Midwesterners attracted to the commercial, social and cultural vitality of New

York, places the narrative in the appropriate perspective of time and space. The novel encompasses a specifically American past and identity, moving all these characters to a point of crisis in which their sense of themselves is threatened. Gatsby, most of all, embodies the duality of American experience, but it is Nick who confronts the issues that this raises.

Notes

1. *The Great Gatsby*: A Novel of the 1920s

1. André le Vot, *F. Scott Fitzgerald, A Biography*, Allen Lane, 1984, p. 177.
2. ibid., p. 107.
3. Matthew J. Bruccoli, *Apparatus for F. Scott Fitzgerald's The Great Gatsby*, University of South Carolina Press, 1974, p. 117.
4. Le Vot, op. cit., p. 124.
5. F. Scott Fitzgerald, *The Great Gatsby*, Penguin; see Note on p. 9 above.
6. Bruccoli, op. cit., p. 131. Certain Chicago White Sox baseball players took bribes to fix the 1919 World Series with the Cincinnati Reds.
7. Le Vot, op. cit., Ch. 9, 'The Underside of Prosperity', covers the historical features in detail.
8. F. Scott Fitzgerald, *The Crack-Up with Other Pieces and Stories*, Penguin, 1965, pp. 9–19.
9. Sleeve of Paul Whiteman record, R.C.A. Victor, D.P.M. 2027.
10. F. Scott Fitzgerald, 'Early Success' (first published 1937), in *The Crack-Up with Other Pieces and Stories*, pp. 59–60.
11. F. Scott Fitzgerald, 'My Lost City', in *The Crack-Up with Other Pieces and Stories*, pp. 20–31. Fitzgerald touches upon a major aspect of America's discovery of itself in the 1920s. Popular entertainment in the form of cinema could make American history a source of mass interest, and jazz and film were establishing America as a source of international culture. D. W. Griffith was a famous pioneer director of silent films, and his *Birth of a Nation* gave epic dimension to a story set in the Civil War.
12. C. Von Pressentin Wright, *New York: Blue Guide*, Ernest Benn, 1983.
13. The American artist Joseph Stella executed the first of his famous paintings of Brooklyn Bridge in 1919. Another, Charles Demuth, was intent upon representing the modern city and his painting 'I saw the Figure 5 in Gold' is a visual image of William Carlos Williams's poem 'The Great Figure', written after he had seen a fire engine rushing down Fifth Avenue. In 1921 an experimental film called *Manhatta* celebrated New York in terms of the geometry of its skyscrapers. The photographers Alfred Stieglitz and Charles Sheeler made New York into a symbol of modernity. Dickran Trajan, *William Carlos Williams and the American Scene, 1920–1940*, University of California Press, 1978, pp. 71–7.
14. *The Letters of F. Scott Fitzgerald* (ed. Andrew Turnbull), Penguin, 1968, p. 571.
15. Malcolm Bradbury and Howard Temperley (eds.), *Introduction to American Studies*, Longman, 1981, p. 199.

16. *Letters of F. Scott Fitzgerald*, p. 182.
17. Quoted in Le Vot, op. cit., p. 101.
18. *Letters of F. Scott Fitzgerald*, p. 500.
19. *Edmund Wilson: Letters on Literature and Politics, 1912–1972* (selected and ed. Elena Wilson), Routledge & Kegan Paul, 1977, p. 64.
20. Other observers were less sanguine. In *Civilisation and the United States* (1922), a symposium by over thirty writers, there was general pessimism about the state of post-war America, and a number of writers were critical of the money-orientated culture the 1890s gave to the 1920s. Robert Emmet Long, *The Achieving of The Great Gatsby: F. Scott Fitzgerald, 1920–1925*, Associated University Presses, 1979. See Chapter 6 of this study for further references to the inheritance of the 1890s.
21. Fitzgerald's final, unfinished novel, *The Last Tycoon*, is concerned with precisely this aspect of the film producer's art in the 1930s.
22. In his introduction to the 1934 edition of *The Great Gatsby*, Fitzgerald suggested that Conrad's novel *The Nigger of the Narcissus* sets forth the terms to be fulfilled by 'a work which aspires to be art'. Quoted in Long, op. cit., p. 86.
23. In *The Modern American Novel*, Oxford University Press, 1983, Malcolm Bradbury makes a useful comparison between these two novels of 1925. Robert Emmet Long notes a third novel of 1925, *Manhattan Transfer* by John Dos Passos, which he describes as about 'the American Dream turned sour' (Long, op. cit., p. 175). Summing up some of the best American fiction of this period in another critical study, Bradbury remarks that the generation of young writers, many from the Midwest, expressed a disillusion caused not least by the war itself, and introduced into their works a strong sense of historical dislocation, of culture displaced, of traditional American values in the process of collapse (Malcolm Bradbury, *The Expatriate Tradition in American Literature*, British Association for American Studies, 1982, pp. 32–3).

2. A Novel of Intricate Patterns

1. Quoted in Andrew Turnbull, *Scott Fitzgerald*, The Bodley Head, 1962, p. 138, from a letter written just before Fitzgerald moved to Great Neck. It defines what he aimed to achieve in his next novel.
2. The word may echo its use in a poem by the famous nineteenth-century American poet Walt Whitman. 'Crossing Brooklyn Ferry' is a sustained lyrical meditation on the continuity of human life and experience which employs the symbol of the ferry carrying passengers between Long Island and Manhattan. The poet envisages others coming after him who will also see the white sails of schooners on 'the scallop-edged waves'.

3. Alternative Worlds

1. 'Two alternative worlds, one of careless wealth and the other of ashen poverty, are hence set in contrast in the novel.' Malcolm Bradbury, *The Modern American Novel*, Oxford University Press, 1983, p. 66.

2. In F. Scott Fitzgerald, *The Diamond as Big as the Ritz and Other Stories* (Penguin), first published in 1925.

3. Trimalchio was a wealthy man who feasted the citizens of Rome, in a satirical poem by the Roman poet Petronius called *The Satyricon*.

4. Again, a reference to Whitman's fine poem may be implicit here. The poet, gazing down into the water from the ferry boat, is dazzled by the sunlight and 'dash'd at the fine centrifugal spokes of light round the shape of my head in the sunlit water'. Whitman absorbs all the minute observations of the scene and transforms them into an acceptance of death and time.

5. 'What shall we do tomorrow?/ What shall we ever do?' T. S. Eliot, *The Waste Land*: 'A Game of Chess', ll. 33–4.

4. The Women Characters

1. *The Letters of F. Scott Fitzgerald* (ed. Andrew Turnbull), Penguin, 1968, p. 197.

2. ibid., p. 507.

3. Judith Fetterley, *The Resisting Reader: A Feminist Approach to American Fiction*, Indiana University Press, 1977, Ch. 3, p. 72.

4. The use of 'his' echoes the opening of Chapter II, but this time it conveys his guests' indifference.

5. A famous German field-marshal in the First World War.

6. '... the sporty Jordan and the conservative Baker electric' (Matthew J. Bruccoli, *Apparatus for F. Scott Fitzgerald's The Great Gatsby*, University of South Carolina Press, 1974, p. 122); that is, the modern, emancipated woman who is determined to enjoy the freedom *and* preserve the advantages of the 'lady'.

7. The point is made by Fetterley, op. cit.

8. He is right. Jordan is the only character in the novel who never needs to fantasize or create fiction about herself or anyone else: for her Gatsby is 'just a man named Gatsby' (p. 50).

9. Presumably in a fashion magazine.

10. These have already been discussed in Ch. 2.

11. See *The Odyssey*, Book XII. The point is made by Glenn Settle in 'Fitzgerald's Daisy: The Siren Voice', in *American Literature*, Vol. 57, No. 1, pp. 115–24.

12. A day particularly associated with her name, which is sometimes interpreted as the 'day's eye, that is, the sun'.

13. John Keats, 'Ode on a Grecian Urn', Stanza II.

14. Daisy's maiden name would seem to imply such an intention on Fitzgerald's part: Fay suggests 'fey' or 'fairy', a magical creature from another world. In Gatsby's imagination she is such.

5. Gatsby and Nick Carraway

1. A battle fought by American soldiers from September–November 1918 (Matthew J. Bruccoli, *Apparatus for F. Scott Fitzgerald's The Great Gatsby*, University of South Carolina Press, 1974).

2. Such a medal existed. Fitzgerald was careful to check facts (ibid., p. 39).

3. A film called *The Young Rajah* was made at this time, but it was so bad it was never released.

4. Bruccoli makes this suggestion, op. cit., p. 119.

5. *The Letters of F. Scott Fitzgerald* (ed. Andrew Turnbull), Penguin, 1968, p. 196. It is worth noting that in the original MS Fitzgerald implied that Gatsby and Wolfshiem were involved in drugs and extortion, squeezing cab-drivers and down-and-outers for money, an explanation that would have reduced readers' sympathy for Gatsby, whereas the final details implicate him in bonds and bootlegging, illegal but not necessarily vicious (Robert Emmet Long, *The Achieving of The Great Gatsby: F. Scott Fitzgerald 1920–1925*, Associated Universities Presses, 1979, p. 189).

6. Drug-stores (chemists) were allowed to sell liquor on prescription during Prohibition, but this served as a front for bootlegging activities (Bruccoli, op. cit., p. 135).

7. In the original MS, but not in the text: '. . . he was a nobody with an irrevocable past, and under the invisible cloak of a uniform he had wandered into a palace'. Quoted in Long, op. cit., p. 183. Note how, in omitting this statement, Fitzgerald condensed the idea more suggestively in the text.

8. 'The orgastic future' (p. 171).

9. See John S. Whitley, *F. Scott Fitzgerald: The Great Gatsby*, Edward Arnold, 1976, p. 57, for a discussion of Nick's moral growth which makes comparison with other literary figures who move towards maturity and self-knowledge through proximity to some charismatic figure.

10. This issue is discussed in terms of American history in Chapter 6 of this book.

11. *The Letters of F. Scott Fitzgerald*, pp. 192 and 199.

6. America: History and Myth

1. *The Letters of F. Scott Fitzgerald* (ed. Andrew Turnbull), Penguin, 1968, p. 188.

2. See the page preceding Chapter I:
> Then wear the gold hat, if that will move her;
> If you can bounce high, bounce for her too,
> Till one cry 'Lover, gold-hatted high-bouncing lover,
> I must have you!'

3. Matthew J. Bruccoli, *Apparatus for F. Scott Fitzgerald's The Great Gatsby*, University of South Carolina Press, 1974, p. 32.

4. 'Orgastic' is printed as 'orgiastic' in some editions. 'Gatsby believed in the

green light, the orgastic future' (p. 171) was meant to express, Fitzgerald said in a letter to his editor, 'the intended ecstasy' (Bruccoli, op. cit., p. 50).

5. A gold rush.

6. In Bruccoli, op. cit., and John F. Callaghan, *The Illusions of a Nation: Myth and History in the Novels of F. Scott Fitzgerald*, University of Illinois Press, 1972.

7. For details, see H. N. Smith, *Virgin Land: The American West as Symbol and Myth*, London, 1970.

8. Quoted by Robert H. Fossum and John K. Roth in *The American Dream*, British Association for American Studies, 1981, p. 106, from James F. Adams, *The Epic of America*.

9. Quoted by E. Fussell in *Frontier, American Literature and the American West*, New Jersey, 1965, p. 13, from 'The Great Nation of Futurity' in *Democratic Review* VI.

10. *Hopalong Cassidy* by Clarence E. Mulford was actually not published until 1910, although it was written in 1907 (Bruccoli, op. cit., p. 138).

11. In a recent television programme on the real city of Dallas a new property millionaire said, '. . . where you can come from nothing and make it big – that's what this country is about'. This is exactly what Gatsby did.

12. *Concise Dictionary of American Biography* (Scribner), p. 15; a recent critic notes: 'The veneration for success and riches had a very central place in the American 1890s and its imaginative literature. Its survival in the era of the 20s is seen in the immense popularity of the Horatio Alger books for boys. Alger published approximately 135 volumes, with titles like *Strive and Succeed* and *Bound to Rise*, in which the setting for fortune-making was transposed from the West to New York city, the modern mecca for success' (Robert Emmet Long, *The Achieving of The Great Gatsby: F. Scott Fitzgerald 1920–1925*, Associated Universities Presses, 1979, p. 174).

13. The very brief section on the novel by Malcolm Bradbury in *The Modern American Novel*, Oxford University Press, 1983, makes illuminating comments on this aspect.

14. Fitzgerald was to create a fictional example of these with the Warren family in his next novel, *Tender is the Night*.

15. A book called *The Rising Tide of Colour* by Lothrop Stoddard was published in 1910. Fitzgerald probably changed the name deliberately (Bruccoli, op. cit., p. 33).

16. In F. Scott Fitzgerald, *The Diamond as Big as the Ritz and Other Stories*, Penguin.

17. Usually assumed to be St Paul, Minnesota, where Fitzgerald himself grew up.

18. Yale, one of the old-established universities, often known as Ivy League.

19. Callaghan, op. cit., p. 50.

20. El Greco (1541–1614) was an artist, Greek by birth, who contributed a major and very personal vision to the great age of Spanish painting. His deeply religious paintings depict figures in a dream-like, visionary style and illuminated by strange light.

21. A recent critic notes that there is a further contradiction in Nick's return to the Midwest where he can keep his moral distinctions straight. It was in this region, in the environs of Chicago, that the Buchanan fortune was made, that Gatsby was closed out of Daisy's life and that Daisy chose Tom. This means effectively that Nick is admitting that 'his' Midwest is an illusion, that he has no alternative place to go to (Long, op. cit., p. 182). In the previous chapter I have argued that by, in effect, becoming Gatsby, after his friend's death, and yet asserting traditional values of friendship and care for the dead, Nick is beginning the process of confronting his own identity. His final vision of the Dutch sailors takes the process further. His journey back to the West is a retreat but it is also a stage of recovery.

Selected Reading

Works by Scott Fitzgerald

This Side of Paradise, Penguin Books, 1963.
The Beautiful and Damned, Penguin Books, 1966.
Tender is the Night, Penguin Books, 1982.
The Diamond as Big as the Ritz and Other Stories, Penguin Books, 1962.
The Crack-Up with Other Pieces and Stories, Penguin Books, 1965.
The Letters of F. Scott Fitzgerald, ed. Andrew Turnbull, Penguin Books, 1968.

Secondary Reading

1. *Works cited in the text*

Bradbury, Malcolm: *The Modern American Novel*, Oxford University Press, 1983. This sets *The Great Gatsby* in a very helpful context of twentieth-century American fiction. The few pages on the novel offer scintillating reading.

Bradbury, Malcolm, and Temperley, Howard: *Introduction to American Studies*, Longman, 1981.

Bradbury, Malcolm: *The Expatriate Tradition in American Literature*, British Association for American Studies, 1982.

Bruccoli, Matthew J.: *Apparatus for F. Scott Fitzgerald's The Great Gatsby*, University of South Carolina Press, 1974. This is a scholarly edition citing all Fitzgerald's textual alterations and offering helpful notes on all references in the text.

Callaghan, John F.: *The Illusions of a Nation: Myth and History in the Novels of F. Scott Fitzgerald*, University of Illinois Press, 1972.

Fetterley, Judith: *The Resisting Reader: A Feminist Approach to American Fiction*, Indiana University Press, 1977.

Fossum, Robert H., and Roth, John K.: *The American Dream*, British Association for American Studies, 1981.

Fussell, E.: *Frontier, American Literature and the American West*, New Jersey, 1965.

Le Vot, André: *F. Scott Fitzgerald, A Biography*, Allen Lane, 1984.

Critical Studies: The Great Gatsby

Long, Robert Emmet: *The Achieving of The Great Gatsby: F. Scott Fitzgerald 1920–1925*, Associated Universities Presses, 1979.

Smith, Henry Nash: *Virgin Land: The American West as Symbol and Myth*, London, 1970.

Turnbull, Andrew: *Scott Fitzgerald*, The Bodley Head, 1962.

Whitley, John S.: *F. Scott Fitzgerald: The Great Gatsby*, Edward Arnold, 1976.

Wilson, Edmund: Letters on Literature and Politics, 1912–1972, selected and ed. E. Wilson, Routledge & Kegan Paul, 1977.

2. *Other Critical Studies*

Eble, Kenneth E.: *F. Scott Fitzgerald: A Collection of Criticism*, McGraw-Hill, 1973.

Hoffman, Frederick J.: *The 20's*, Macmillan, 1965.

Miller, J. E.: *F. Scott Fitzgerald, His Art and His Technique*, New York University Press, 1964.

Perosa, Sergio: *The Art of F. Scott Fitzgerald*, Ann Arbor, 1965.

Sklar, Robert: *F. Scott Fitzgerald: The Last Laocoön*, Oxford University Press, 1967.

Stallman, Robert: *The Houses That James Built*, University of Michigan Press, 1961.

Stavola, Thomas J.: *Scott Fitzgerald: Crisis in American Identity*, Vision, 1979.

Stern, Milton R.: *The Golden Moment: The Novels of F. Scott Fitzgerald*, University of Illinois Press, 1970.